D1196346

The Psychology of Dyslexia
A handbook for teachers

Dedication

To all the teachers at East Court School and those on the
Dyslexia Institute Diploma course 1999/2000

The Psychology of Dyslexia

A handbook for teachers

MICHAEL THOMSON, BSc, MSc, PhD, CPsychol,
FIARLD, AFBPS

Principal, East Court School for Dyslexic Children
Honorary Senior Lecturer in Applied Child Psychology at the
University of Kent

Consultant in Dyslexia
PROFESSOR MARGARET SNOWLING
University of York

LIBRARY
FRANKLIN PIERCE COLLEGE
RINDGE, NH 03461

W

WHURR PUBLISHERS
LONDON AND PHILADELPHIA

© 2001 Whurr Publishers
First published 2001 by
Whurr Publishers Ltd
19B Compton Terrace, London N1 2UN, England and
325 Chestnut Street, Philadelphia PA 19106, USA

All rights reserved. No part of this publication may be
reproduced, stored in a retrieval system, or transmitted in any
form or by any means, electronic, mechanical, photocopying,
recording or otherwise, without the prior permission of
Whurr Publishers Limited.

This publication is sold subject to the conditions that it shall
not, by way of trade or otherwise, be lent, resold, hired out, or
otherwise circulated without the publisher's prior consent in
any form of binding or cover other than that in which it is
published and without a similar condition including this
condition being imposed upon any subsequent purchaser.

British Library Cataloguing in Publication Data
A catalogue record for this book is available from the British
Library.

ISBN: 1 86156 248 9

Printed and bound in the UK by Athenaeum Press Ltd,
Gateshead, Tyne & Wear

Contents

Acknowledgements

Thanks are due to Wendy Goldup at the Dyslexia Institute (DI) who was the organiser of the Tonbridge DI Diploma course 1999–2000. Thanks also to the teachers on that course who gave valuable feedback on the quality of my overheads and handouts upon which this book is based. Thanks also to Martin Turner, Head of Psychology at the DI, for encouraging me to use my lectures as a basis for a book.

The structure of this book and how to use it

Please read this!

The purpose of this book is to present the underlying psychology of dyslexia to, mainly, teachers who may be undertaking a training course on teaching children with dyslexia. The book will also be of interest to parents of dyslexic children, teachers who are already trained and want to brush up current knowledge and teachers who have dyslexic children in their class.

The book grew out of the once-weekly lectures on psychology that I gave to the Dyslexia Institute's Diploma in Specific Learning Difficulties in the 1999/2000 academic year. I have tried to make the style accessible, with tables and diagrams wherever possible. Inevitably there are references and complex arguments to be taken into account, but I have tried to provide an overview of the essentials, with further reading suggested.

Content and structure

The content broadly follows the psychology syllabus of 'Dyslexia Teaching' diplomas and certificates. The following topics are specifically covered.

Chapter 1:   The nature of dyslexia as a syndrome and its historical context: descriptions, education acts.

Chapter 2:   Basic psychometrics: how psychological and educational tests are constructed; standard scores, validity, what tests measure.

Chapter 3:   How dyslexia is assessed: ability, attainment and diagnostic tests given by psychologists; how to interpret reports; what tests teachers can use; case history, examples.

Chapter 4:   Current issues on diagnosis of discrepancies between intelligence, attainment, phonological skills and assessment.

Chapter 5:   Basic neuropsychology: brain function/language areas; auditory and visual processing; hemisphere function.

Chapter 6:   Neuropsychology of dyslexia: genetic predisposition; cerebral dominance; laterality; EEG brain imaging; dichotic listening; written language functions, cerebellar and visual transient theories.

Chapter 7:   Models of reading and spelling: nature of written language; stage models of development; skills needed to acquire written language.

Chapter 8:   Models of memory, particularly working memory and its relationship to reading skills.

Chapter 9:   Phonological and memory skills in dyslexia: notion of core phonological deficit; memory difficulties.

How to use the book

The reader will note from the above that some chapters are basic psychology topics whereas others focus on dyslexia. Unless the reader is familiar with psychology, it is suggested that the basic knowledge chapters are read first, followed by the 'dyslexia' chapters.

As it is unlikely that the reader will take in the whole book at one sitting, I have deliberately sandwiched dyslexia chapters between the basic psychology. Each chapter forms a coherent (I hope!) whole, equivalent to two or more lectures. Each chapter could be read independently but here are two suggestions for reading the book.

1. Reading individual subject basics followed by the relevant 'dyslexia' section. This follows the order of the chapters in the book, i.e. Chapter 1, then 2, 3, 4 (assessment), 5, 6 (neuropsychology), 7, 8 and 9 (cognitive).
2. Reading all 'basics' followed by all 'dyslexia': Chapter 1, then 2, 5, 7, 8 (basics), then 3, 4, 6 and 9.

Alternatively, completely ignore the above and read from page 1 to the end or any other way you want!

Why have I organized the book like this

It seems to me that the first stage of understanding dyslexia is to recognize children who have dyslexic difficulties. This implies observation and, crucially, assessment, Before reading psychologists' reports and undertaking your own assessments, it is important to understand the assessment process, hence the first four chapters.

I have then divided the aetiology of dyslexia into two broad areas: its biology and the cognitive expression of the underlying neuropsychology. This division essentially follows the model given in Figure 1. This is my adapta-

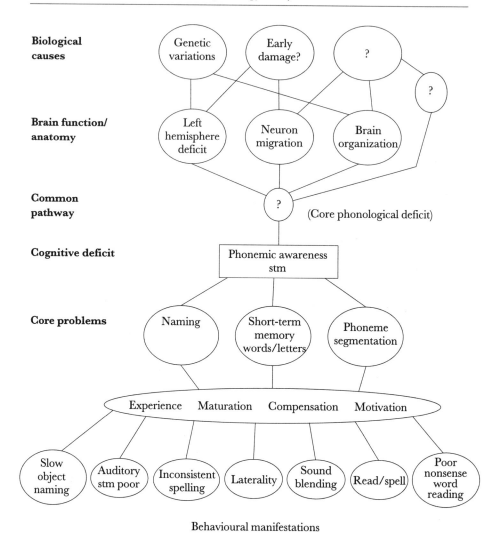

Figure 1 Model of developmental disorders. (Adapted from Frith, 1992.)
stm = short-term memory.

tion to dyslexia of a developmental model put forward by Frith (1992). She has since extended this to look at different theories of aetiology and these are the 'models of deficit' in the dyslexia chapters.

At the bottom of Figure 1 are the observable characteristics of dyslexia entitled 'behavioural manifestations'. The features listed here are examples of those typically observed in dyslexic children. We examine and list these in more detail in Chapter 1.

Although there are some commonalities, each child brings his or her own experience, particular received teaching, level of difficulty, etc.

However, there is a common pathway to the syndrome. If we start at the top of Figure 1, you can see suggestions of biological causes linked to brain function and anatomy. These issues are discussed in Chapters 5 and 6. There is then a hypothesized common pathway. These result in cognitive deficits and core problems which are discussed in Chapters 7, 8 and 9. The cognitive builds on the biological basis, hence the position of the neuropsychology chapters first.

CHAPTER 1

The nature of dyslexia

Emergence of a syndrome

Although many books and papers refer to the case histories of Hinshelwood (1900) and Morgan (1896) describing word-blind children and the recognition of acquired dyslexias from the beginning of the century, it was not really until the 1970s that dyslexia has been recognized as a specific learning difficulty in this country. Similar developments have taken place in other parts of the world, particularly the USA.

In the UK in the early 1970s, the 1944 Education Act was still in force. Basically, this argued for a number of categories of handicap, in which dyslexia and specific learning difficulties were not included. If you did not fall into one of these categories, you officially did not exist, and therefore the notion of dyslexia did not exist.

What we might call 'barriers to learning', i.e. factors that were seen to prevent children from acquiring literacy, fell into broad categories of problems which were seen to be either extrinsic to the child, e.g. to do with society and school teaching, or intrinsic, i.e. within the child, which were to do with intelligence and gross neurological problems.

A typical child guidance centre at the time, to which children were referred if they had a variety of educational difficulties including problems with reading, included a psychiatrist, an educational psychologist, a social worker and a teacher. Problems were very broadly viewed within social background, and intellectual and emotional spheres.

As far as social background was concerned, Table 1.1 shows the typical finding (Eisenberg, 1966) of the relationship between presented reading difficulties and socioeconomic class.

The fact that children of a lower socioeconomic status background had more difficulties reading and spelling was seen to be the result of factors such as linguistic background, perceptual experience, attitudes from home towards school, etc. For example, it was felt that, if parents had fewer

1

Table 1.1 Percentages of children with reading difficulties in different occupational classes

Class	Percentage
1 and 2	7
3	19
4 and 5	27

educational qualifications, the implication was that they discouraged their children from seeing school work as important and the children picked up that view. If there was a restricted use of language or less richness of environmental experience at home, this might prevent a child being ready to acquire written language learning. Programmes such as Head Start (which gave us Sesame Street and the Muppets!) and others were all geared towards making a child ready to acquire reading, writing and spelling.

As far as the intellectual sphere was concerned, it was recognized that there was a good correlation between intelligence and reading ability. Children were categorized, based on intelligence test scores, into those who might fall into the 'educationally subnormal' or the 'severely subnormal' categories, which reflected the Education Act categories of handicap. Children typically falling within these cut-offs might be referred for education in special schools. In later chapters we examine in great detail this relationship between intelligence and reading and discrepancy models of dyslexia.

If there were no explanations to be found within the child's social background (social worker) or his or her intellectual profile (educational psychologist), then an explanation was sought within the emotional sphere. Here, children might be perceived to be emotionally disturbed, which was preventing them from acquiring written language learning. The response to this might be either drug therapy or, if the child was perceived to have particular psychiatric problems, through play therapy at the child guidance centre.

There was, therefore, a reasonable set-up for identification of children in the above areas. However, many teachers were still commenting on children who, despite not showing any of the above so-called barriers to learning, were still not acquiring reading, writing and spelling. Early identification of dyslexia was therefore based on descriptions by teachers and others working in this area, as well as exclusionary definitions. In other words, if a child was intelligent, came from a well-supported home background, did not have a primary emotional problem, but was still failing to read, write and spell, he might be described as dyslexic.

There were, at the time, a number of these descriptions or symptomatologies and these are still produced. The British Dyslexia Association, the Dyslexia Institute, the Hornsby Centre and many other well-known organizations working in dyslexia all produced their own lists of 'symptoms'. A typical example of this is given in Table 1.2.

Other associated factors may include: late language development and continued pronunciation difficulties; ambidexterity or mixed handed-

Table 1.2 Features of dyslexia

A puzzling gap between written language skills and intelligence

Delayed and poor reading and spelling, often with persistent reversals and disordering of letters, syllables and words (d/b, was/saw, place/palace)

'Bizarre' spelling (raul/urchins, kss/snake, tars/trumpet) and others that are more recognizable (wayt/wait, pant/paint, boll/doll)

Confusion of left/right direction

Sequencing difficulties such as saying the months of the year in order; poor directional scan in reading; weak sequential memory

Poor short-term memory skills (repeating digits; following complex instructions)

Problems in acquiring arithmetical tables

Problems in repeating polysyllabic words (sas'tis'ti'cal for statistical, per'rim'min'ery for preliminary)

Difficulties in expressing ideas in written form

From a booklet produced by East Court School (1983, 2000).

ness; similar problems in other members of the family; clumsiness; poor graphic (writing) skills; and dyspraxia.

We can make this a little more concrete by looking at case histories and examples of actual and hypothetical children. Let us look at 'Charlie', shown in Figure 1.1.

Charlie is a young man aged 11 years who has just started his secondary school and is dyslexic. On the left-hand side are a number of characteristics that are similar to those in other children of his age, and on the right-hand side and the bottom are a number of characteristics that are different from those of other children. The right-hand side shows those skills that Charlie does less well than his peers, and at the bottom are those items that he might do rather better than his peer group.

If we look at Charlie himself, we get some clues about some aspects of dyslexia. He is looking rather worried and anxious. He has not been sleeping very much. This results partly from the fact of starting a new school where he is rather lost. Children with dyslexia sometimes have difficulty with orientation, and he finds it very difficult to know where he is at any given time. Particularly important, he finds it difficult to read his timetable. This is a very long and complicated document. He is not sure whether he is supposed to be reading it across the top or down the side,

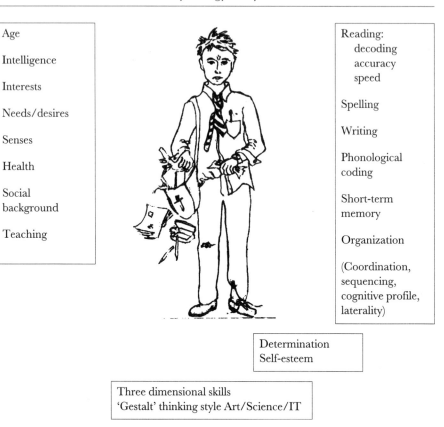

Age		Reading:
		  decoding
		  accuracy
		  speed

Intelligence		
Interests		Spelling
Needs/desires		Writing
Senses		Phonological coding
Health		
Social background		Short-term memory
Teaching		Organization
		(Coordination, sequencing, cognitive profile, laterality)

Determination
Self-esteem

Three dimensional skills
'Gestalt' thinking style Art/Science/IT

Figure 1.1 'Charlie', a dyslexic 11-year-old.

and does not understand the abbreviations. He also finds it difficult to read some of these. As a result of this, he not only has problems in finding out where he is supposed to be, but he does not know what lessons he is having either in the morning or in the afternoon on a given day. To solve the problem, he takes all the books he needs for all of his classes around with him! This results in a huge bag full of all the books and papers that he needs. Inevitably, as a result of his weak organizational skills, a lot of the contents fall out. You will notice that he is carrying lots of pencils because he forgets them and doesn't want to get into trouble for losing them. He often gets shouted at by teachers or told off for not having the right materials or equipment at any given time. As he has weaknesses in short-term memory, and this forgetting is inevitable.

Many, but not all, children with dyslexia are somewhat more clumsy than their peers, and therefore he has problems in doing up his tie and his shoelaces even at the age of 11. At the present time, he is looking at his watch, not just to see what time it is but actually to work out which direction is left and which right, as he has been told to go down the left-hand corridor, followed by the right-hand corridor, straight along for two or three doors, and go up the stairs and turn left towards the science block where he will find his next lesson! He has problems in processing all this information as well as, of course, remembering it. It is not surprising that he is looking worried and lost!

On the left-hand side are things in which he is similar to other children. He is the same age as the other children and he is of the same general intellectual background. It is a misnomer to say that all dyslexic children are intelligent – sometimes reported erroneously in the media. It is obviously easier to spot a dyslexic child if his attainment skills are well below his intelligence. Nevertheless, people with dyslexia have just as wide a range of intelligence as the rest of the population. He may be bright, he may be less able on intelligence tests or he may be of average ability. Charlie's interests are the same as those of other children. Currently, as I write, these are scooters and 'yo-yoing' at my school, but there will be something different next term, I am sure. He has the same needs and desires – he wants to be successful, he needs to be loved, he needs to be secure, he needs to have all those things that make a child of 11 feel comfortable and happy in his environment and school.

By and large his senses are the same as those of other children – he can see (he might have glasses, he might not) and on the whole he can hear well. There may have been some slight hearing losses when he was younger – grommets and such like – which are often more common in dyslexic children. Charlie's health, social background and the received teaching he has had are all the same as for other children, and yet he has problems in reading and spelling.

On the right-hand side are the things with which he has difficulty. Obviously dyslexic children are seen to have problems with reading, but we should note here that this is not all aspects of reading. If we are able to help the dyslexic child work out what the words are in reading, his comprehension can be quite good. The problem is not in higher order skills – we shall be looking in some detail at these later – but in decoding the words; so decoding, accuracy and speed of reading are all weak, as are spelling, writing, phonological or sound coding, short-term memory and the other items listed. We look at all of these in more detail later (see page 121). Sometimes dyslexic children will have problems with coordination, sequencing, language and laterality. Again, we examine all of these in greater detail (see page 80).

At the bottom of the diagram are areas that some people with dyslexia do well on. My clinical, research and teaching experience suggest that many people with dyslexia are rather better at three-dimensional skills, i.e. they have what we might term 'gestalt' thinking. Within the families one gets good skills in engineering, architecture, dentistry, medicine, art, design, etc. At school they tend to do rather better at Science (the experimental part, not the copying from board and writing!), Art and IT. An anecdote that I have written elsewhere illustrates this point. Some time ago we had a craze for remote-controlled cars at the school, and I bought a kit for one of my own children (but, in reality, to make for myself!). I tend to be a very linear thinker and I like to read the instructions and follow step 1, step 2, etc. After months of trying to construct this model, burning the midnight oil, I still could not make it work. One day I brought it over to the school and the children looked at the cogs and gears and said 'You've got them all the wrong way round, Sir!' and like magic rearranged the whole of the gearing so that it worked. They were able to look at the exploded diagram, understand the spatial relationships involved and how the whole thing worked, and construct it in that way – a much more relevant skill than mine. Of course, I am lucky that linear/verbal skills tend to be tapped in the early part of a child's school career as opposed to those skills that many people with dyslexia have, which tend to be in the visualization and three-dimensional area.

You will notice that Figure 1.1 talks about self-esteem and determination. Children with dyslexia who are not given help have very low self-esteem and we also look at this in a little more detail later. However, given the right sort of help they can build up a strong determination to succeed. If they can overcome the 'I am dyslexic and I can't do it' approach, they can do very well. Again, our experience is that many of our children who go on to their senior schools can do rather better at 'A' levels than their non-dyslexic peers. This is because, if you have never had a problem with reading and spelling in education, you sail through your GCSEs with no problem. There is a big gap between GCSE and 'A' level standard. Some students find it very hard work and are not sure how to deal with it. The child with dyslexia who has been given good study skills and knows how to work, metaphorically says 'Oh, more hard work – no problem' at 'A' level and just gets on with it.

To return to the main theme of this first chapter, the general realization of dyslexic problems tended to be based on descriptions of children such as Charlie and symptomatologies as listed in Table 1.2. I do not propose to present a whole series of case histories here. There is a psychometric case history in the next chapter which will be referred to when we look at assessment, but many books give case histories, my own (Thomson, 1990) and many others included. I would assume that the reader will be familiar with such books; the purpose of this book is to look at the underlying psychological constructs of dyslexia.

The next development in recognition of the dyslexia syndrome was the Government Green paper, the Tizard Report (1972). This was based on the Isle of Wight study of Rutter, Tizard and Whitmore (1970). The Isle of Wight was taken as a representative sample of the social background of the UK and a number of educational, social and medical details were looked at. A brief technical digression is needed here. This study, along with that of Yule (1967) and Yule et al. (1974), examined the relationship between intelligence and reading in the general population, using regression equations. Regression here refers to the interrelationship of variables, in this case between intelligence and reading, and what they were able to do was to make a prediction of what a child's reading and spelling should be like, based not only on his chronological age but also on his intelligence. The reader should not confuse 'regression' as a correlation with 'regression to the mean'. This is the tendency for population characteristics (e.g. height or intelligence) to tend towards the average of that population. We shall be examining this later when discussing discrepancy models, but there is this potential confusion based on the technical terms used in statistics and psychometrics.

The following is an example of a regression equation, looking at the relationship between reading and intelligence, which predicts reading accuracy for a child of a given age:

Reading accuracy = 3.87 + (0.93 × IQ) + (0.68 × CA).

Here, the IQ refers to the sum of the scaled scores from the short form of Wechsler's Intelligence Scale for Children (range 4–76, average 40) (Wechsler, 1992) and the reading is the Neale Analysis Accuracy score in months (Neale, 1997). (The chronological age or CA is also in months.) The other figures were derived from the way in which reading and intelligence were correlated in that particular population. For any individual child in the Isle of Wight, therefore, and also when they undertook similar work looking at the effects of lead on IQ in the then Inner London Education Authority, we can look at what their expected reading should be. On the basis of this, they found that children could be divided into those who had a general reading difficulty (e.g. a 10-year-old who had an IQ of around 80 and who might be reading at the 8-year-old level), and those who had a specific difficulty (e.g. a 10-year-old who had an IQ of 115 and would be expected to be reading at, say, the 10.5-year-old level but who was only reading at the 8.5-year-old level). We look at this issue in more detail when we look at criticisms of the notion of discrepancy and its actual use in educational psychology practice nowadays (see page 47). However, Rutter et al. (1970) presented data that showed the differences between those children with general reading difficulties and those who had specific reading difficulties. These are presented in Table 1.3.

Table 1.3 Children with general and specific retardation

General	Specific
Mean IQ 80	Mean IQ 102
General development delays	Speech/language delays
54% male	76% male
Better prognosis	Very poor prognosis
Overt neurological deficits: e.g. 11% cerebral palsy, etc.	No organic, fewer neurological deficits
High incidence of large families	Lower incidence of large families
High number of low status homes	Low number of low status homes

It may be seen that those with a general reading difficulty had general developmental delays, i.e. late in walking and talking, came from social backgrounds that might be expected to cause problems in literacy learning, and had more neurological dysfunctions that were organic. However, the children with specific difficulties had only language/speech delays; there were many more boys than girls, and their problems were much more to do with reading and spelling rather than general educational failure. The children with specific difficulties were also more difficult to help, despite, on average, being brighter, in other words they make less progress in reading.

Based on the above, the Green Paper identified children who had 'specific reading retardation'. Those of us working in dyslexia at the time said: 'These are the dyslexic children.' We also argued that, because dyslexia was not just about reading but included spelling, difficulties in writing and a number of other things, some of which we have delineated in Charlie and some of which are tabled later in this chapter, there was a considerable overlap between these groups. However, at least this was the first official recognition that there were children who had specific difficulties, and it laid the foundation for an acceptance of dyslexia as a learning problem.

Moving on very rapidly in the development of dyslexia as a concept, we pass the Warnock Report, and to date with the abolition of the 1948 Education Act and the introduction of the Special Educational Needs Acts of 1981, 1983 and 1994. Here statutory assessments have taken place, giving rise to a Statement. Special Educational Needs are defined as a learning difficulty requiring special educational provision. This involves a learning difficulty, which can be defined as the following:

1. There is significantly greater difficulty in learning than for others of the same age.
2. Disability prevents or hinders use of educational facilities for children of the same age in local education authority (LEA) schools.
3. If a child is aged under 5 years, (1) and (2) would apply if the child were at school.

There are a number of key features in this list that should be examined. One is that these are essentially normative assumptions – in other words, there is some recognition that a child is being compared with his peer group, and there should be some expectations of what 'normal' children should be doing at a given age. This is important because it implies some form of psychometric analysis and comparing children across norms, something that is very variably applied in schools and by educational psychology practice. Also there is an implication for some developmental context, i.e. we are looking at children changing and developing over time – a key feature – as children learn and grow. Finally, there is an underlying assumption that these learning difficulties are preventing a child from accessing the curriculum. Table 1.4 shows how the Special Educational Need Act applies to a dyslexic child.

Table 1.4 Code of Practice with regard to a specific learning difficulty

i.   There are extreme discrepancies between attainment in different core subjects of the National Curriculum or within one core subject, particularly English/Welsh. LEAs should be especially alert if there is evidence that, within the core subject of English/Welsh, a child has attained average or high levels in Attainment Target 1, speaking and listening (oral in Welsh), but significantly lower levels in AT2, reading, and/or AT3, writing.

ii. Expectations of the child, as indicated by a consensus among those who have taught and closely observed him or her, supported, as appropriate, by appropriately administered standardized tests of cognitive ability or oral comprehension, are significantly above his or her attainments in National Curriculum assessments and tests and/or the results of appropriately administered standardized reading, spelling or mathematics tests.

iii. There is clear, recorded evidence of: clumsiness; significant difficulties of sequencing or visual perception; deficiencies in working memory; or significant delays in language functioning.

iv. There is evidence of problems sometimes associated with specific learning difficulties, such as severe emotional and behavioural difficulties, as indicated by clear, recorded examples of withdrawn or disruptive behaviour, an inability to concentrate, or signs that the child experiences considerable frustration or distress in relation to his or her learning difficulties. LEAs should be particularly alert if there is evidence of such difficulties in some classes or tasks such as reading or writing but not in others.

We now have a situation in which children are defined as having special educational needs and, if we look at the Code of Practice, specific learning difficulties is one of these.

Before finishing this chapter, it is useful to look at some of the other features of dyslexia that are not subsumed by the LEA notion of 'specific learning difficulty'. Tables 1.5 and 1.6 show some comments that reflect a dyslexic child's difficulties, both at home and at school.

Table 1.5 Some difficulties facing children with dyslexia around the school

Organization	– timetables; homework and assignments; completion of work
	– finding the way around school
	– personal organization
	(– parents' organization!)
Coordination	– ball games: cricket/squash, etc. for some (see below)
	– fine motor vs gross motor skills
Note-taking	– from blackboard
	– from dictation
Project work	– extraction of information from source
	– time to complete assignment

Positive features

Good skills in:	– work effort and determination
	– global 'gestalt' thinking; logically applied, sometimes maths
	– computer studies
	– CDT, including technology/design/art skills/engineering
	– games ability, namely 'balance', three-dimensional skills
	– science, especially experimental laboratory skills, but see note-taking!

Table 1.6 Difficulties shown by the dyslexic child around the house

Disorganization
Bedroom – tidiness, etc.
Planning life – events, times, activities
Out and about on own – buses, finding way
Time keeping!

Memory
Homework
Objects/clothes
Events/time keeping!
Instructions

Personal
Hair/teeth/dressing!
Attitude to others
Homework!

Most of the features mentioned in Tables 1.5 and 1.6 are self-explanatory, but some comments may be helpful. Children with dyslexia will often miss out on assignments, resulting partly from short-term memory difficulties because the teacher quickly says, at the end of the lesson as the children are leaving, something like 'Oh yes, homework on Wednesday, Chapter 6, pages 29 to 35. Don't bother with question 3, and by the way use last week's notes for question 2 and don't forget I want at least a page of summary at the end.'

There will be similar problems in copying from the board and speed of work as a result of difficulties with visual memory (board to book) and speed of processing. Children with dyslexia may be still on an earlier piece of work when the teacher is moving on or giving out instructions! Note the comment about parents. It is easy to blame parents for not helping children to organize themselves, but they may also be dyslexic – in fact this is highly likely, given the genetic predisposition that occurs.

In Table 1.6 there is a reference to attitude to others. This can refer to taking it out on a younger sibling who can read, as well as other secondary reactions to a primary learning difficulty that I explore in later chapters.

Finally, a comment on the severity of reading, writing and spelling difficulties in children with dyslexia. Going back to Table 1.3, one of the important differences between the general and specific retardations was the prognosis. Despite being of generally higher intelligence, children with specific learning difficulties made less progress in reading, writing and spelling in a follow-up study undertaken in the Isle of Wight. If we look at what children with dyslexia can be expected to achieve without being given help, we find something rather like Figure 1.2.

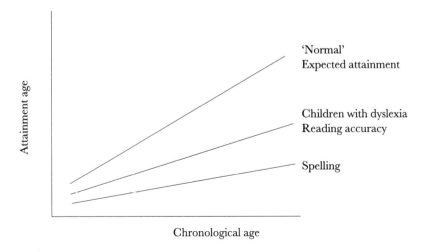

Figure 1.2 Observed attainments in dyslexic children.

These data are taken from the University of Aston and have been presented elsewhere (Thomson, 1990), but they are essentially from a cross-sectional study, which shows children's performances seen on assessment for the first time and at various different age levels thereafter. Obviously, one would normally expect children aged 8 years to be reading at the 8-year-old level, those aged 9 to be reading at the 9-year-old level, and so on, in which case one would get a straight graph. This is, of course, on average (children and adults do vary, and what is 'normal' can be debated at length!). Children with dyslexia who are not given help make, on average, progress of 5 months in reading per year and of 3 months in spelling. Thus, as they get older they get further and further behind in reading, writing and spelling. What may be a 1-year retardation at age 7 becomes one of 3 or 4 years at age 10 and of 5, 6 or 7 years at age 15. The whole notion of 'don't worry, children will grow out of it' is something we need to resist. Our task as educators is to stop that gap widening, and ideally to increase the rate of the reading and spelling improvement so that children get up to a competent standard of literacy.

Further reading

For a detailed overview of the historical context of dyslexia see the following:

Miles TR, Miles E (1998) *Dyslexia 100 Years on*, 2nd edn. Buckingham: Open University Press.
Pumfrey PD, Reason R (1991*)* Dyslexia. *Specific Learning Difficulties*. Windsor: NFER–Nelson: Chapter 1.
Thomson ME (1990) *Developmental Dyslexia*, 3rd edn. London: Whurr. Chapter 1.

CHAPTER 2

Basic psychometrics and assessment

The next three chapters look at the process of assessing the child with dyslexia, from the point of view of both the educational psychologist and the teacher. The aim of these chapters is to give the reader an understanding of the way in which tests are constructed and how they are used, how educational psychologists assess children, how to interpret reports and test results given by psychologists, and finally how to assess dyslexic children themselves.

Before looking at the underlying theory and practice of test construction, I think it would be helpful to present a 'psychometric case history'. This is essentially a list of typical tests that might be given by an educational psychologist to provide a flavour of the kind of diagnostic assessment criteria that might be used. This chapter then looks at how tests in general are constructed and further chapters look in detail at tests of ability, attainment and other diagnostic tests that are relevant to dyslexia.

A brief case history

This case history, which we examine in more detail in the next chapter, gives us a picture of a child with an average (107) Full-Scale IQ derived from using the Wechsler Intelligence Scale for Children – III (WISC-III: Wechsler, 1992). Table 2.1 and Figures 2.1 and 2.2 present the test results following assessment. The child has an average Verbal IQ with a Performance (Non-Verbal) IQ in the above-average range. It is also noticeable that, if we look at the individual subtests on this test, there are some low and some high scores. Figure 2.2, in particular, illustrates this and it can be seen that Information, Arithmetic, Digit Span and Coding are rather lower than the other tests. We discuss the implications of this later (see page 21), but suffice it to say at this point that, using an individually administered intelligence test, we can come to some general measurement of intelligence as well as look at the specific cognitive profile of the child. We can also look at

Table 2.1 Case history: test results

This boy had been receiving extra help for his reading and spelling at school. Despite this, he was not making progress. He was referred for a full assessment to obtain a psychological and educational profile. The assessment was undertaken to look at the possibility of obtaining a Statement for him and providing him with some help for his written language difficulties.

Chronological age (years;months) 10:9

Intelligence and ability

Wechsler Intelligence Scale for Children III
Full-Scale IQ = 108

Verbal IQ = 103

Performance IQ = 113

Subtests

Information	8	Picture completion	13
Similarities	14	Coding	7
Arithmetic	6	Picture arrangement	12
Vocabulary	12	Block design	14
Comprehension	13	Object assembly	13
(Digit span	5)		

Index scores

Verbal comprehension	110
Perceptual organization	120
Freedom from distractibility	74
Processing speed	83

Attainments

	Age-related score (years/months)	Predicted standard score	Actual standard score	Difference
WORD				
Basic reading	7.09	104	76	$p < 0.001$
Spelling	6.09	104	68	$p < 0.001$
Reading comprehension	8.00	105	80	$p < 0.001$

Neale Analysis of Reading Ability

Accuracy	7.11
Comprehension	8.06
Rate	6.07

Indicative reading and spelling errors

Reading errors included *sad* for *said*, *aminal* for *animal*, *sole* for *slow*
Spelling errors included *ct* for *cat*, *fis* for *fish*, *gup* for *jump*

Free writing

Very little writing attempted, slow non-fluent vocabulary and expression weak compared to oral language. Six words per minute.

Further diagnostic tests

Graded Non-Word Reading Test	7.00 equivalent
Phonological Abilities Battery	Problems with both beginning and end deletion of phonemes

some general learning styles, e.g. the Index Scores shown in Figure 2.1 give Verbal Comprehension and Perceptual Organisation in the range of average to above-average, whereas Freedom from Distractibility and Processing Speed are rather below average. Again, what these imply is discussed later (see page 38) and later in this chapter we also look at how such indices and

WISC-III/WORD quotient and discrepancy analysis.

	Expected score based on IQ and age	Actual score	Comments
Basic reading	104	76	$p < 0.001$
Spelling	104	68	$p < 0.001$
Reading comprehension	105	80	$p < 0.001$

Figure 2.1a Intelligence Indices and WORD quotients.

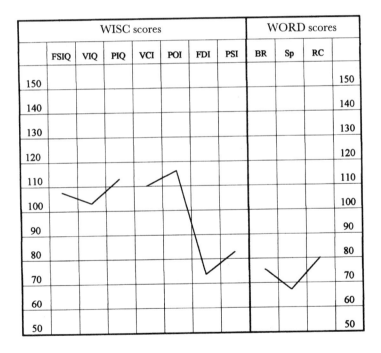

Key:

FSIQ	Full-Scale IQ	FDI	Freedom from Distractibility Index
VIQ	Verbal IQ	PSI	Processing Speed Index
PIQ	Performance IQ	BR	Basic Reading
VCI	Verbal Comprehension Index	Sp	Spelling
POI	Perceptual Organisation Index	RC	Reading Comprehension

Figure 2.1b Profile scores.

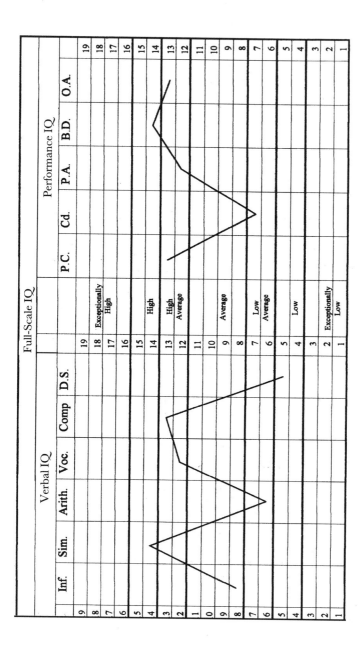

Key:
Inf = Information; Sim = Similarities; Arith = Arithmetic; Voc = Vocabulary; Comp = Comprehension; DS = Digit Span; PC = Picture Completion; Cd = Coding; PA = Picture Arrangement; BD = Block Design; OA = Object Assembly.

Figure 2.2 Case history: WISC-III scaled scores profile analysis.

test scores are derived in test construction. This is important because sometimes the labels that are given to such test results do not necessarily reflect what is going on in the individual child!

This case history also presents some basic data on age-related scores in reading, spelling and reading comprehension, and predicted standard scores. We looked at examples of this in Chapter 1, and here we have specific examples where the difference between the predicted and the actual standard score in reading, spelling and comprehension is significant, with the child having very poor scores on attainments. Similar results can be observed using the Neale Analysis of Reading Ability as well as the Wechsler Objective Reading Dimensions (WORD: Wechsler, 1993), which is specifically linked to a discrepancy analysis. We therefore now have a further point to look at – the notion of a discrepancy between written language attainments and age incorporating some expected attainment based also on intelligence. This has recently been considered to be controversial in some quarters, but is well established in educational psychology practice and will continue to be used by those working in dyslexia, I have no doubt. Figure 2.3 demonstrates how IQs can be plotted as well as indices and compared with scores on written language attainments. We also look at the notion of how to plot graphs and alternative ways of doing this in the next few chapters. Figure 2.3 repeats the discrepancy scores given.

We now have some indications of intelligence and attainment. What the case history does not give is any detailed breakdown of reading and spelling behaviours, although there are some indications of reading and spelling errors which, again, are typical for children with dyslexia. Finally, there are two 'diagnostic' tests, including a non-word-reading test, which looks at the ability to decode letters without their meaning, and part of a phonological abilities test, which looks at phonemic awareness – in this case, the ability of the child to deal with sounds at the beginning and end of words. In Chapters 3 and 4, we look at these three areas – intelligence, attainments and 'diagnostic' tests. We shall be refering to this case history in the next chapter, but for the remainder of this chapter we look at some aspects of test development, so that the reader is aware of the advantages and disadvantages of using tests, and particularly the understanding of important concepts such as error of measurement, ability and reliability, etc.

Introduction to testing

Psychological testing has a background of individual differences in psychology. Essentially, tests may measure the difference between individuals or within the same individuals, e.g. on different occasions. A psychological or educational test is simply a means of measurement and, as we shall see, the names given to tests are sometimes quite arbitrary and do not necessarily reflect accurately the underlying cognitive or behavioural traits that they purport to measure.

It is also important to consider what kind of level of measurement a particular test has. Traditionally, in statistics and psychometrics in psychology, there are three types of measurement – nominal (e.g. boys/girls, children with/without dyslexia), ordinal (ranking data, comparing individuals with others – fifth in class, 30th centile), and finally interval (which attempts to give an absolute value, e.g. quotient of 112 or 17/25 on a test). An interval score with children usually has an implication of relative value. This is because a test that gives a quotient, centile or other score will usually have been standardized on children of different ages. This implies that a good score for a 10-year-old, for example, may be a poor score for a 13-year-old, and that individual development needs to be taken into account.

A test may be defined as an objective and standardized measure of a sample of behaviour. It is objective because the same result should be obtained every time that it is given, and it is not based on someone's subjective opinion of another person's ability. It is standardized because it is given in the same way every time. This is essentially what instructions for tests are all about and it is important to follow them carefully. It is also standardized because it may have been tried out on a large sample of individuals. Finally, the notion of a sample of behaviour is important. It is only a snapshot of a person's given behaviour at that particular time. There are many other variables that may account for this behaviour, and therefore there is always a built-in error of measurement. This error can be quantified, as we see later (see page 30). It is very important to remember that a test is only a small sample of an individual's behaviour. It gives us a guide and no more; we return to this point later. For the teacher, it is only really a starting point in trying to evaluate a child's cognitive, educational and other skills, with the fundamental purpose of trying to teach them in a better way.

The test is usually based on a small but carefully chosen sample of individual behaviours, e.g. in developing a Vocabulary Scale we might choose a representative sample of words for different ages. These words are then tested out on many individual children and only those tests that differentiate different age groups, for example, would be chosen for the final Vocabulary Scale. A test should have diagnostic or predictive value, i.e. it should indicate broad significant areas of behaviour that we are trying to tap. It should ideally be able to predict future behaviour. There is also usually a close parallel between the test itself and behaviour, e.g. between the knowledge of a word list in a vocabulary test and mastery of vocabulary in language use.

There are many different uses of tests. They can be simply a description of individual differences, but they can also measure qualities of human behaviour or describe them operationally, e.g. intelligence or anxiety. They are often used in making practical decisions about people or predictions. Examples include: identifying mental handicap; diagnosing the reason for attainment failure in children; identifying variables in an experiment and describing the effect of 'treatments'; in vocational guidance, selection or assessment and many other uses in occupational, clinical and educational psychology. Table 2.2 gives examples of different types of tests.

Table 2.2 Examples of different types of tests

Achievement/attainment (of ability, aptitude); specific/general abilities	Reading, e.g. General: Neale Analysis of Reading Ability Specific: British Ability Scales Word Reading
Intelligence (general mental ability)	Wechsler Intelligence Scale for Children
Special aptitudes	Phonological Abilities Battery
Personality (trait/projective)	Trait: Eysenck's Personality Inventory Projective: Rorschach 'Ink Blot'

Standardization of tests

There are two aspects of standardization. One is how a test is given and the second is how it is constructed. As far as the first is concerned, it is important to produce uniformity of procedure in administration of the test. In other words, the same test should be given to all individuals. The only independent variable should be the individuals being tested.

It is important, then, in learning to use tests that you become totally familiar with the materials and the oral instructions. The number of demonstrations that should be given to the person being tested are important to develop the right set or approach to the test. Another important aspect is timing – this can present quite a problem even in a relatively 'simple' test such as the Neale Analysis of Reading. Here we need to listen to children reading (and make notes on errors and approach to reading), time them carefully and, finally, ask questions at the end of each passage. Sometimes, when starting to use a test, we can easily lose track of all these different aspects, and it is important to practise the test many times before giving it to an individual, when it is 'important'.

The objective is that all examiners should give the same assessment. However, another important element that is very difficult to quantify is that of rapport. If a child is not feeling well, does not like the examiner, is unhappy, or is feeling low because of a bad playground experience or any other factor, then we are not going to get a very reliable or valid test. It is very important to make a child feel relaxed, motivated and alert with the aim of maximizing an individual's performance within the constraints and standardization of the way in which the test should be administered. Spending some time chatting to children and putting them at their ease is an absolute must, and a warm, friendly atmosphere is important. Children should not feel that they are being examined in a punitive way. With this in mind, a child's performance on a test is really only a basal level.

This rapport and eliciting, i.e. drawing out a child's best performance without giving him the answer, are difficult for some teachers. Occasionally teachers may find themselves wanting to tell the child the answer or help him, which of course is not allowed within a test situation. Unfortunately some teachers are so used to dealing with children in a large group that their personal individual skills may be a little rusty and they can come across as a little formal and pedagogic. If you feel that you cannot achieve good rapport with an individual child whom you are testing, it may be wise to ask a colleague to undertake the testing for you.

However, it is my experience that, with the right practice and guidance, teachers can become excellent testers, particularly if they are going to be following up teaching that child, in the case of dyslexia, because the psychometric profile is only the start. Diagnostic teaching is a very important, if not the most important, component in the total picture of a child's learning process.

The second type of standardization refers to how the test has been developed in other populations. In general, tests are either norm-referenced or criterion-referenced. A norm-referenced test compares the score to that of other similar individuals, usually belonging to the same age groups in the case of children. It is not the ideal performance, but depends on levels of difficulty. To take a concrete example, if we had a word reading test of 50 items, it might be a good performance for a child aged 10 years to read 15 of these, whereas if a child aged 6 read 15 items it might be an excellent performance; conversely, a child aged 13 reading only 15 items might be rather weak. Obviously, this means that the test items have to be standardized and tried out on large samples of children. It is important, therefore, to make sure that the tests have been standardized over appropriate groups. This also leads us to the notion of standardization samples. In other words, on what population was the test standardized? If a test is to be used widely, it should show in its manual a wide variety of social backgrounds and geographical areas.

In general, tests are constructed to be normally distributed, and later in the chapter we look at this concept; it may, however, depend on the type of discrimination between individuals or within individuals that is described on a particular test. The idea is to compare (in the case of children – the main focus here) with the general peer group. The way in which this is done is often by standard score, Z scores or percentiles. We will look at these in detail, because they are crucial to our understanding of what test results are, whether we undertook tests ourselves or interpreted other people's reports.

The other standardization type mentioned above is the 'criterion reference'. Here there is an absolute score rather than a relative one comparing other children. It has become more popular recently, particularly in education. The question here would be: Can an individual define 20 words or not? We set a particular criterion and the question is whether the child can or cannot do it. This has often been used and developed into Individual Education Plans in the case of dyslexia, e.g. a goal could be the criterion of the child reading and spelling 10 consonant blends. This is thus an assessment and a teaching goal. Of course, the problem is specifying the so-called 'ideal performance' and whether the objectives be clearly stated and agreed on.

Evaluation of tests

The question here is: 'How good is the test, and does it actually work?' The first component of this is reliability.

Reliability

It is important for a test to be reliable, i.e. do we achieve consistent scores? Ideally, the same individual using the same test on a different occasion should give us the same score. Obviously, individuals are not like blocks of wood to be measured exactly by physical means. People's behaviour intrinsically varies from day to day (especially children's!) and there is always some in-built error within the test. Psychometricians recognize this and develop an error of measurement in the individual score. This is the chance of 'irrelevant to the test' factors. The test is essentially an estimate of the so-called 'true' characteristics of the individual – their moods, day-to-day changes, personalities, testing conditions, examiner, perceived importance of the test, etc., will all affect the result and, of course, error variance. It will also depend on standardization conditions and the sample, i.e. the normative sample, on which the test has been standardized. We look at error of measurement and its relationship to the spread of scores later (see page 28), but it is important to recognize here that the reliability or coefficient stability is the same as a general correlation coefficient, i.e. it ranges from −1 through 0 to +1. Just to remind the reader, a correlation coefficient is the relationship between two variables, e.g. there is a high positive correlation between people's height and the size of their feet, although there is usually a negative correlation between rainfall and temperature in the UK, i.e. the higher the rainfall, the lower the temperature. Usually a high positive correlation is needed for a test to be reliable, i.e. one of +0.8 or so.

There are various types of reliability, as follows.

Test–retest reliability

This involves correlating the test over time. Of course, in children this is difficult to do because they are learning and developing. A test–retest would therefore rarely exceed 6 months in the case of children. However, there are also problems in practice and recall effects, so simply retesting a person on the same test as a measure of reliability tends to be used less often in practice.

Alternative form

This usually compares two different forms of the same test, e.g. the Neale Analysis of Reading has two forms. The forms are developed in parallel and measure the same thing. Reliability is thus compatibility between parallel forms.

Internal consistency

This looks at the correlation between test items, e.g. in a vocabulary test of, say, 20 items, items 1–2, 3–4, etc. are correlated and internal consistency is measured.

Scorer reliability

Here again, we should get the same score on a test for the same individual even though it was given by different people. This is more likely in simple objective tests, e.g. reading individual words, but is less likely in clinical and subjective tests. Tests that require interpretation are also less reliable.

Basically, the reader needs to look at the test manual to see whether there is evidence given about the reliability of the test. Does the test produce the same results on different occasions and with different testers? It is important for there to be a high positive correlation for the test to be considered reliable.

Validity

The other important aspect of test construction is what the test measures and how well it tests. The test name usually gives a general guide, but it is not always completely clear, e.g. in reading we could test accuracy, speed, comprehension, single word reading, reading individual letters, understanding stories, etc.

Sometimes, factor analysis is used to give tests their labels. Factor analysis is basically a multiple correlation with different tests or different measurable behaviours. A good example of this was given in our case history at the beginning of the chapter. The WISC-III gives us Index Scores, which are given labels based on the intercorrelation between the test items. So, for example, Information, Vocabulary, Comprehension and Similarities (a verbal reasoning test) are put together as the Verbal Comprehension Index. (See page 37 for a description of these subtests.) They are linked together because they are correlated highly in objective testing of many children. However, the label was one based on what it was assumed the tests measure. It is important to recognize that sometimes test labels are only the results of correlational links and the assumed underlying cognitive processes that they measure. Intelligence is a good example of a label given to a set of behaviours that correlate well (although they do have other validities), but are open to philosophical, technical and psychological debate.

However, to return to validity, we can look at a number of different kinds of validity as follows.

Face validity

This is what the items appear to measure and can be important to the individual, e.g. a reading test usually has words to read! This is not as fatuous as it sounds, because sometimes we may find a very high correlation between a test and later behaviour, e.g. there is a good correlation between rhyming ability at 5 or 6 years and later reading and spelling development, so if we gave a rhyming test to a 5-year-old we could argue that it measured aspects of reading ability, although that would be difficult to justify to a parent who might say: 'Why didn't you give a reading test?'

Content validity

This is 'Does the test include a representative sample of the behavioural domain?'. The question, of course, is still posed in the reading example: 'What aspects of the behavioural domain?' There may be over-generalization, e.g. in spelling should we include a multiple choice spelling or words written down from dictation or words used in writing as the measure of spelling? All are equally valid but measure different things.

Criterion-related validity

This is perhaps the most important validity and it looks at whether the test is linked to the direct independent measure to which purports, e.g. if we used a test to select a person for a job, does high performance on the test predict good performance later in the job? In early occupational psychology, a well-known mistake occurred in which police officers were rejected on the grounds that they did poorly on a particular selection test. Later the occupational psychologist tested successful policemen, and found that they also did very poorly on that test; therefore it was not a very good predictor of future performance and not valid as a selection procedure. In other words, does the test relate to real-life behaviour, i.e. the criterion.

There are basically two types: predictive and concurrent or diagnostic. Predictive validity asks the question: 'Does the test predict future performance?' A good example of this is when I was developing the Aston Index (Newton and Thomson, 1976). We tested children at 5 years and went back to the same children 2 or 3 years later to see which test items predicted their later reading and spelling development. That was predictive validity, e.g. poor scores on Sound Blending linked to later reading difficulty. In addition, there was a correlation of 0.83 between Sound Blending at age 5 years and reading level (Schonell Reading) at 8 years.

Concurrent validity asks the question: 'Does the test correlate well with present performance, or do particular groups of people score well or poorly?' Again, in the Aston Index example, we tested children aged 8–12 years and looked at those who had reading and spelling difficulties to find out whether they also scored less well on items of the Index. There are various criteria that can be used to evaluate either predictive or concurrent validity, e.g. academic achievement, performance in training, previously available tests, job performance, contrasting groups and, of course, educational success at school.

Construct validity

This refers to the psychological state, process or trait being measured, and looks at the relationship between the test and the theory. We should be able to predict from the theory what the test should measure.

Table 2.3 gives examples of different kinds of validation which should make the above clearer.

Scoring tests

We now look at another element of psychometrics, i.e. the kinds of scores derived from the test. This is important because often tests have different

Table 2.3 Types of validation on, for example, Arithmetic Reasoning Test

Purpose	Example question	Type of validity
Achievement in primary school	How much has Fred learnt? (or what learnt?)	Content
Aptitude to predict secondary school achievement	How well will Fred learn in the future? (or will he do well on Maths course)	Criterion related – predictive
Technique to identify/ diagnose arithmetic difficulties	Is Fred 'dyscalculic'?	Criterion related – diagnostic (concurrent)
Measure of logical reasoning	How can we describe Fred's psychological functioning?	Construct

kinds of scores, and it is essential to understand how they are derived and what they mean. Perhaps I should mention in passing here that, as well as the establishment of rapport and getting the optimum performance from a subject, it is imperative to check one's personal accuracy using stencils and keys, and to be consistent and careful in the way that we score tests. These can be important factors in children's lives and it is essential to get it right. It is also important to respect the confidentiality of material, as well as the fact that the test is only one element of a child's total profile.

Obviously, the raw score itself is only a numerical report of performance and has no significance unless it is compared with some standard. We cannot interpret psychological tests as we do physical measures. Differences in, for example, reasoning ability do not present true differences between individuals, unless we know their background, age, etc. The raw score is therefore converted into some kind of derived score, i.e. a permanent record of the individual's relative position. There are two main kinds of derived scores – centiles and standard scores. It is perhaps worth presenting at this point a normal distribution and aspects of score systems that will give rise to these (Figure 2.3).

Centile scores

A centile or percentile score is a rank expressed in percentage terms. A percentile is a way of expressing a large number of people in a rank order score. Therefore, a percentile or centile of 88 means that an individual is better than 88% of the population and worse than 12% on that particular test. Conversely, a centile of 40 means that an individual is better than 40% of the population or worse than 60% of the population. One of the

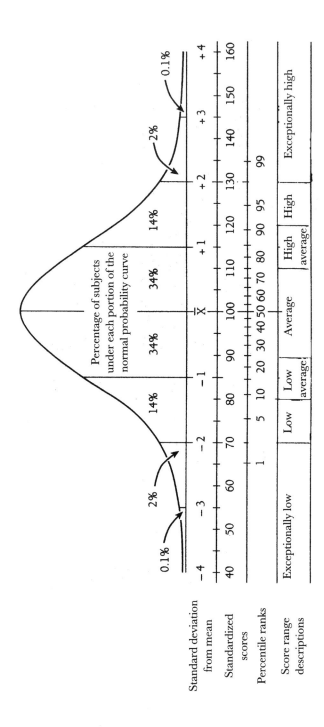

Figure 2.3 Normal distribution and associated score systems.

advantages of percentiles is that they are relatively easily understood and give a fairly exact interpretation with no gaps in the raw score (they are also psychometrically easy to compute in test development). One of the problems, however, is that they do magnify small differences near the mean. If we look at Figure 2.3 one can see that the average range for percentiles lies between 25 and 75. The descriptions of score range used on Figure 2.3 are similar to the Wechsler classification. They may differ slightly from test to test, but the principles and statistical range will be the same. This means that a percentile of 40 is not reliably worse than a percentile of 60. They are all within the average range and therefore there is no real difference between a centile of, say, 45 and 55. Centiles apparently give an indication that there is a difference here, and that is very important to understand in their interpretation. Conversely, there is a reduction in the size of large differences near the tail ends of the distribution. If we look at the normal distribution in Figure 2.3 and compare, say, the 90th with the 99th centile, we can see that there is only a very small percentage of the population (under the curve) scoring in that area. What this means statistically is that a small difference between 90 and 95 (or 10 and 5 at the lower levels) makes a great deal of difference in terms of the test scores for those individuals. Thus the difference of five centile points is very significant at the extremes, whereas it is of little significance between 50 and 45 or 50 and 55. This is an important statistical point that is sometimes ignored and is one of the problems of using centiles.

Standard score

A standard score indicates a person's place in the frequency distribution of the test. We can look at an example of a standardized score, i.e. the so-called Z score. This is computed by looking at the individual's score and looking at the standard deviation (spread) of the scores, e.g. if John gets 22 for an arithmetic test and the others get 12, 14, 12, 14, 14, 17, 19, 11, 15 and 20, the mean or average score is 15.4. The standard deviation or spread of score is 3.42 (we look at this concept later – see page 30). Therefore John's standard, or Z score, is:

$$\frac{X - M}{SD} \quad \text{i.e.} \quad \frac{\text{his score} - \text{mean}}{\text{standard deviation}} \quad = \quad \frac{22 - 15.4}{3.4} \quad = 1.9.$$

This Z score, therefore, which has a mean of 0 and a standard deviation of 1, can be compared from test to test. It is also important to recognize that one can transform a Z score so that the mean is 100 and the standard deviation is $10(Z \times 10 + 100)$. This is essentially what has happened when, as is the case in many tests, a quotient with an average or mean of 100 is set and we look at deviation scores or quotient scores such as IQ, British Picture Vocabulary Test (BPVT), and some reading and spelling tests (see pages 39 and 40).

Before looking at alternative standard scores, it is important to understand the concept of standard deviation. Standard deviation is essentially the variability of a particular random score. Figure 2.4 (two normal distributions) shows two examples of populations, i.e. individuals who have been given tests and the scores have been added up.

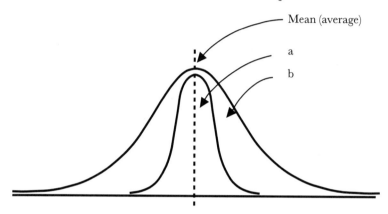

Figure 2.4 Normal distribution of the populations. See the text.

In one situation (a) with the narrow bell-shaped curve there is a very narrow range of scores; and in the other (b), with a wide bell-shaped curve, there is a wide range of scores. Note that the same average, or mean, applies. In the first case most of the individuals have scored at around the same level, whereas in the second case there have been a very wide variety of scores. The standard deviation is essentially just a statistical measure of this variety or spread of score.

What test constructors do is essentially assume that their tests are normally distributed (or, better still, base them on the standardization sample on which they have developed the test). There are, therefore, a number of standard scoring systems that you will come across in your interpretation of tests, and some of these are shown in Table 2.4.

If we compare Table 2.4 with Figure 2.3 showing the normal distribution, we get an idea of the different standardization systems. In the case of the Wechsler scores given, these refer to the individual subtests (see Case history on page 14, for example). Here the mean, or average, is set to 10 and the standard deviation is at 3. Note that examples are given with *one* standard deviation above the mean and *two* standard deviations below the mean.

Table 2.4 Standard score systems

Mean set equal to	Standard Deviation set equal to	Standard Score corresponding to 1 SD above mean	Standard Score corresponding to 2 SD below mean	System
0	1	1	−2	Z scores
5	2	7	1	Stanine score
10	3	13	4	Wechsler subtests
50	10	60	30	t scores
100	15 or 16	115 or 116	70 or 68	Quotient/deviation

This is just to show the reader the score variations – try to work out scores with 2 SD above and 1 SD below for further illustration. Therefore, on the WISC, an individual scaled score of 13 would be *one* standard deviation above the mean, whereas a scaled score of 4 would be *two* standard deviations below the mean (7 would be 1 SD below the mean). The other examples given are the *t* scores, which are used in the British Ability Scales, but the most common is the mean set to 100, the so-called deviation score, which is used for IQ and a number of other tests. Again, looking at the standard deviations above and below the means will give some idea of what these scores actually mean statistically.

It may be seen, therefore, that standard scores give proportional differences to the raw scores and make more sense statistically. They can also give easy comparisons across tests and they do not have the magnification of small mean differences and reduction of large differences shown by the centiles. However, they can be difficult to understand, as may be seen from the above, and do rely on a normalized distribution.

Attainment ages

Another common form of standardization used in education is the attainment age. This would give a reading or spelling age, which is readily understood and easy to use to compare children with each other. However, a further word of caution here because, if we take on board all that has been said so far, it is clear that 1 or 2 months is not a significant difference in terms of test measurement. To say a child who has a reading age of 9:6 is reading better than a child with a reading age of 9:3 is not reporting a reliable difference, a point that we shall make even clearer when we look at the way in which error can be measured (see page 30). Similarly, if we convert reading ages or other attainment ages into centiles or standard scores, it gives us a better idea of whether a child is within a normal distribution. Table 2.5 presents some examples of reading ages compared with other scores from the Weschler Objective Reading Dimentions (WORD) to give a flavour of how important it is to understand these elements in interpreting test scores, and how ages and scores vary.

Table 2.5 Examples of different reading test scores for 10-year-old chronological age based on different raw scores on WORD Basic Reading

Raw score	Reading age (years;months)	Standard score	Percentile rank
40	10:3	99	47
18	6:6	70	2
51	17:0	120	91
37	9:3	94	34
47	14:0	113	81

As far as age is concerned, we can also develop a quotient score by looking at mental age over chronological age, as the Stanford–Binet test did when first developing intelligence tests. We could do the same thing by dividing a reading or spelling age by chronological age to give a quotient score, but again this should be used very cautiously and it is better to look at the standardization scores from the test itself.

Standard error

As we have mentioned before, it is possible to measure the standard error of tests, and many tests do give this in their test manuals. The standard error of measurement is computed by the following formula:

$$\sigma_{meas} = \sigma \sqrt{(1 - R_{11})}$$

where σ = SD of test and R_{11} = reliability
e.g. IQ test SD 15 and reliability 0.89, σ_{meas} = 5 (from $15\sqrt{(1 - 0.89)}$ = $15\sqrt{0.11}$ = 15(0.33) = 5). Thus an IQ of 100 is in the range 95–105.

To rephrase that, in the example of an IQ test with a standard deviation of 15 (see Table 2.4) and the reliability of the test is 0.89, we have a standard error of measurement of 5. Therefore, if a person scores at an IQ of 100, the range of scores is between 95 and 105.

The next bit is where many teachers I have talked to hold up their hands in horror and say, 'Well, what is the purpose of giving tests at all?', and that is when we look at confidence limits. A confidence limit looks at how sure we can be that the test scores achieved are a 'real score', i.e. they do actually reflect what that individual person does. Confidence levels look at what the percentage of a score is at various standard deviations (see Figure 2.3). We know, for example, that 68% of scores on a given test lie between +1 and −1 standard deviation from the mean (34% below and 34% above the mean). Therefore this, in the example that we looked at above, gives a 0.68 probability of the measured IQ of 100 being between 95 and 105. This is derived from our standard error of measurement which we computed at 5 (see above), and the range is 5 either side of 100. The confidence limit is computed by multiplying the standard deviation (in this case 1) by the standard error of measurement (in this case 5). Another way of expressing this is that there is a 2 to 1 chance (68 : 32) of our score being a 'correct' one. If, on the other hand, we wanted to be 99% sure of our score, we would have to look at the 99% of scores on a normal distribution. Here we find that 99% of the scores lie between +2.58 or −2.58 SD (again see Figure 2.3). Therefore the confidence limits are computed by multiplying the standard deviation by the standard error of measurement, which in this case is $2.58 \times 5 = 13$. So our score of 100 ranges between 87 and 113 if we are looking at a 0.99 chance of the real score being within these levels.

Therefore our score of 100 has various ranges depending on how confident we are, in statistical terms, about the test. This is why psychologists report that average scores for intelligence lie between 90 and 110, because this is the confidence range.

Please note that we are talking about statistical confidence here, not necessarily confidence about whether the test is measuring what we want it to measure. A typical limit for reading age in a test such as the Neale Analysis of Reading in some months either side of the observed, e.g. Raw Score 53, Reading Age 9.00, 68% confidence band, gives 8:7–9:11. Note that, these confidence limits are based on the reliability of the test. Despite these caveats on attainment tests and confidence limits, I must reiterate that I as well as many psychologists and teachers still use attainment tests as a good indicator of the child's achievements. They provide a guide to attainment but, as with all tests, are a 'snapshot' of the child's skill.

We have only skated over the surface of some of the technical issues involved in psychometrics (the reader may feel that we have gone too deep!). It is now time to move on to the realities of the test situation and to describe the assessment process for dyslexia in more detail.

Further reading

Anastasi A (1988) *Psychological Testing*, 6th edn. New York: Macmillan.

Aitkinson RC, Atkinson RC, Smith F, Bem D (1993) Assessment of mental abilities. In *Introduction to Psychology*, 11th edn. Orlando, FL: Harcourt, Brace Jovanovich.

Cronbach (1984) *Essentials of Psychological Testing*, 4th edn. New York: Harper Row.
Murphy KA, Davidshofer OC (1991) *Psychological Testing. Principles and Applications*. Englewood
    Cliffs, NJ: Prentice Hall.

The above are basic texts that provide more detail on psychometric theory and practice. For a (slightly dated) overview of different forms of practical assessment try:

Mittler P, ed. (1976) The *Psychological Assessment of Mental and Physical Handicaps*. London:
    Methuen.

CHAPTER 3

Assessing the dyslexic child

In this chapter we look at the assessment procedure for identifying children with dyslexia. I hope, by the end of this chapter, to enable readers to be more confident in interpreting an educational psychologist's report, and also in understanding what tests and what interpretations they can make from these tests in their own assessments.

The focus of the chapter is a case history, which I present, of a child whom I assessed myself. The reader needs to refer to the details in Chapter 2 (page 13). This, I hope, serves two functions. One is to bring about an understanding of an educational psychologist's report; I go into some detail here, particularly about the intelligence test items, which are tests that are closed to teachers and given only by psychologists. Second, at various points I refer to examples of tests that might be used by teachers in order to obtain similar profiles. From time to time, I discuss side issues pertaining to dyslexia or referring to other parts of the book that expand these issues in more detail. I hope that the reader is able to get a general feel of the assessment procedure from this.

The purpose of assessment is, of course, not only to give a diagnostic description of a child, whether in terms of 'dyslexia' or of a 'specific learning difficulty', but also partly to include a delineation of his or her particular strengths and weaknesses. The aim is to develop appropriate remedial teaching on the basis of this. As I have said assessment is only the start because teaching also needs to be diagnostic. Observation, particularly in terms of the response that a child makes to your own teaching, is an important element of the diagnostic and assessment process.

In general terms, the case history presented has been divided into three types of test: first the intelligence or ability tests, second the attainment tests and finally the diagnostic tests.

Intelligence tests

I think that the evaluation of intelligence is an important element of the assessment of dyslexia and I have gone into this in some detail elsewhere (see Thomson, 1990), but let us look here at the specific examples given in the case history (see Table 2.1).

The first aspect is the general, overall IQ. If a teacher is looking at a quotient obtained by an educational psychologist, or not obtained by yourself using alternative tests, it is important to recognize the variability of performance within individual children. The previous chapter examined standard errors of measurement and aspects of the reliability and validity of tests. However, what we can say in this case is that this is a boy with a Full-Scale IQ of 108 who is therefore of at least average ability. I say *at least* average ability because some scores are low and some higher. The Full-Scale IQ is an average. We look at the implications of this later.

In other words, the reading and spelling difficulties of the child do not appear to result from a slow learning potential but, more importantly in this context, they are used as a baseline to evaluate the relationship between his reading and spelling performance and that predicted on the basis of intelligence. This is an important issue that I have examined in Chapter 4, because there are some quite detailed arguments to take into account.

Having said that the child is of average ability, the next stage is to look at his Verbal and Performance or Non-Verbal IQs (103 and 113, respectively). Here there is a slight discrepancy between the two, although this does not reach statistical levels in terms of the Wechsler Manual. This discrepancy between Verbal and Performance intelligence would give us a guide as to whether there might be serious language problems in the child's profile. If the Verbal scale were very poor, we might refer the child to a speech and language therapist or undertake some more complex language assessment processes. Conversely, if the Performance IQ were weak, we might suspect some potential motor problems and perhaps ask an occupational therapist or others to look at the possibility of a dyspraxic difficulty. Of course, these are very crude suggestions and we need to look in much more detail at the subtests of the scale. These are arranged under both Verbal and Performance or Non-Verbal items. They consist of 11 items: 6 Verbal and 5 Performance. The Digit Span subtest is given in brackets because this test is not usually used to compute IQ.

As we have seen from Chapter 2, the Wechsler Scaled Scores have a mean of 10. If a child has a Scaled Score of 10 on all of the 10 items used to compute IQ, he or she would obtain an IQ score of 100. We see here that there are a number of items that are rather weaker than the other tests. These are the Information, Arithmetic and Digit Span on the

Verbal scales, and the Coding on the Non-Verbal scales. These scores from two other children are plotted in Figure 3.1. One can see that these particular tests, when rearranged, give us the so-called ACID profile (Arithmetic, Coding, Information, Digit). This is sometimes linked to children with specific learning difficulties, and the evidence is reviewed elsewhere (Thomson, 1990). However, there are a number of issues we need to explore at this point. Figure 3.1 shows two profiles. A brief description of these tests is given later along with a discussion of the implications of an 'ACID' profile.

The shaded profile shows a child with a Full-Scale IQ of 108, Verbal IQ of 109 and Performance IQ of 107. The solid profile is a dyslexic child with a Full-Scale IQ of 99, a Verbal IQ of 97 and a Performance IQ of 107. There are a number of issues here, and they also refer to our core case history. The first is, what is the true IQ of the child with dyslexia? Both in the case we are considering and in Figure 3.1, an IQ is given by averaging out all of the subtests. Is this an appropriate way of dealing with IQ? If there are some very specific weaknesses, as there often are in dyslexic children, is it fair to include these as part of the IQ when, as we

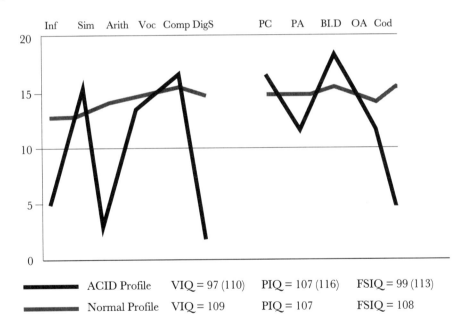

Figure 3.1 'ACID' and normal WISC profiles. The scale on the left is scaled scores, with 10 being the average.

The abbreviations are as follows: Arith, arithmetic; Bl D, block design; Comp., comprehension; Cod, coding; Dig S, digit span; FSIQ, Full Scale IQ; Inf, information; M; OA, object assembly; PA, picture arrangement; PC, picture completion; PIQ, Performance IQ; Sim, similarities; VIQ, verbal IQ; Voc, vocabulary.

see later, some elements of these particular tests are fundamentally linked to dyslexic difficulties. It is rather like evaluating a dyslexic child's intelligence on the basis of whether or not he or she can read.

In contrast, if we excluded any child's really very poor scores from IQ evaluation, is this also a fair estimate, given that tests have been standardized on large populations, and these particular tests may be elements of the definition of intelligence?

Sometimes, if I am reporting test scores, I might include scores in brackets that are pro-rated (a legitimate scoring system I can use in the Wechsler Scales) without the use of the very low subtest(s). Certainly I would discuss in detail in the report the fact that this intelligence test item was very weak, and therefore the overall IQ given may be only an underestimate of what the true performance. We return to this when we look at Index scores later (see page 38).

It is also important to look at the way in which the individual subtests tell us something about the child's intelligence profile.

Table 3.1 gives a brief description of all the WISC intelligence test items, and we can see how these are a reflection of different aspects of a person's cognitive skills.

With regard to the ACID profile in Figure 3.1, Information is simply a general knowledge test. If you had problems with reading, you could imagine losing out on picking up information and general knowledge. Also there are quite a few items, particularly in the early stages of the test, that are specifically 'anti-dyslexia loaded'! These include the direction in which the sun sets, naming the month that comes after March, etc.

The other tests tap particular cognitive skills such as short-term memory, phonological skills and others, which have been summarized by Miles and Ellis (1981) as being difficult for children with dyslexia, e.g. Arithmetic is really a bit of a misnomer because items are given orally. The child has to carry numbers across the 10 barrier and undertake tables that are notoriously weak in children with dyslexia. The test has elements of short-term memory and attentional focus skills, and is not really tapping into arithmetic. Dyslexic children may often forget the question, although they may have been able to do the computation itself if it was written down. Digit Span is a test of auditory sequential memory or aspects of phonological working memory which, again, is often found to be weak in children with dyslexia, as we see in later chapters looking at aetiology that examine both memory and phonological decoding (see page 122). Finally, Coding is a test that is particularly tortuous for children with dyslexia! Essentially, the test involves serial scanning, short-term memory, graphics skills and processing speed, all of which tend to mitigate against children with dyslexia.

Table 3.1 Brief description of WISC subtests

Verbal scale	
Information	This is a test that measures the extent of the child's general knowledge and his or her ability to recall information from long-term memory (VC)
Similarities	This is a measure of abstract verbal reasoning. The child says the commonalities between two words, e.g. apple/banana (VC)
Vocabulary	This is a test of the child's understanding of words. Words given orally must be defined (VC)
Comprehension	This test measures understanding of everyday situations, including 'commonsense' and social reasoning (VC)
Arithmetic	This is a test of mental arithmetic, involving a range of cognitive functions including short-term auditory working memory (FD)
Digit Span	This is a measure of short-term auditory working memory. Numbers are repeated so sequential memory is also involved (FD)
Performance (non-verbal) scale	
Picture Completion	This is a visual perception task where the child has to find missing parts in a picture (PO)
Picture Arrangement	This is a visually presented sequencing task. Story-like cartoon sequences must be rearranged correctly (PO)
Block Design	This is a test of spatial imagery, three-dimensional problem-solving ability and visuomotor coordination. Blocks must be rearranged to match a shown pattern (PO)
Object Assembly	This is a jigsaw puzzle-type task, requiring skills of reasoning, long-term visual memory and visuomotor coordination. Pieces are put together to make an object (PO)
Coding	This is a measure of short-term visual memory, speed and visuomotor coordination. Children must copy specific symbols against numbers as fast as possible (PS)
	Letters in brackets refer to the Index Score to which the subtest loads:
Index scores *(see later discussion)*	VC = verbal comprehension PO = perceptual organization FD = freedom from distractibility PS = processing speed

In contrast, my experience shows that children with dyslexia do rather better at tests such as Block Design, Object Assembly, Picture Completion, in which there may be involvement of three-dimensional or visual observational skills.

Before examining the Index scores, a brief comment about the ACID profile is needed. It is my experience that many dyslexic children have this profile, but not all by any means. It is not the only diagnostic criter-ion, and the recent British Psychological Society (BPS) Working Party (1999) on assessment of dyslexia argued that the ACID profile is not as frequent as has been assumed in dyslexic children. Nevertheless, it is more common and a great deal of research looks at profiles examining general means between populations of children with and those without dyslexia where there are significant differences on these subtests. The mean scores of the 300 plus children who have attended East Court School over the last 17 years show this profile very clearly. Again, these studies are reviewed in Thomson (1990). Suffice it to say here that there is a difference between general population studies and individual performances. In the assessment diagnostic case, we want, of course, to look at a particular individual performance.

If we look at the Index scores on the case given, we find that there is a considerable discrepancy if we group some of the subtests together. We discussed previously how difficult it is to give appropriate labels to scores that have been developed from factor analysis or intercorrelation.

The Verbal Comprehension Index score is taken from the Information Similarities, Vocabulary and Comprehension subtests. If we look at our case history again (see page 14), we find a boy who is in the above-average range for the sorts of skills typically associated with school learning. You may think the difference between 107 and 110 is not significant and you would be right statistically and operationally. However, the dreaded 11+ test still operates where I work and it can be very important for me to point out to schools and local authorities that a particular child does well at Verbal Comprehension skills if he or she is coming up to the test. Here a small difference in quotient points is seen to be highly significant by the authorities. They are indeed significant in terms of the child's future educational – indeed, life – experience, based on some arbitrary cut-off point or statistically invalid criteria. However, let us return to the main point in question before I get too carried away with criticizing the 11+!

The next Index score is the Perceptual Organization score. In our case history, this indicates that the boy has above-average skills in these areas (117). This is commonly associated with dyslexic individuals in my clinical and research experience, and is essentially to do with three-dimensional and spatial skills. It is unfortunate that these tend not to be evaluated at school, in the sense that they are skills associated later in life with engineering, design and visual skills. On the other hand, some dyslexic children, particularly those who have dyspraxic difficulties, often do less well on these tests because they are very strictly timed. If they have problems in manipulating the blocks or in putting the parts of the jigsaw puzzle-type task together, it will affect their performance because they will not get bonus points for quick time.

The other two Index scores are good examples of tests that have been given labels that do not, in my opinion, totally explain what they are to do with. The Freedom from Distractibility and Processing Speed indices are typically weak in children with dyslexia, and in our case history they are no exception (quotients 74 and 83, respectively). The Freedom from Distractibility Index, however, comes from the Arithmetic and Digit Span subtests. Certainly there is an element of attentional focus in doing well on these tests, but there are also other elements, such as embedding of arithmetic skills within sentences and language on the Arithmetic subtest, and short-term memory on the Digit Span subtest. Children who have the label 'hyperactivity' or 'attention deficit disorder' do not necessarily always do poorly on these tests, and many children with dyslexia who could in no way be described as having an attention deficit do less well on both tests, as mentioned previously. Finally, the Processing Speed index is essentially the Coding subtest and involves elements of visual recognition, serial scanning and graphics skills, to name just a few, as well as speed of processing, obviously. Figure 2.1 (see Chapter 2, page 15) presents the general IQ scores and the Index scores graphically, along with the three attainment tests given from the Wechsler scales.

It is hoped that the above gives some insight into the most commonly used individually administered intelligence test by educational psychologists, the Wechsler Scales. The British Ability Scales is another test that is widely used, and that will also have weak scores in Speed of Processing and Short-Term Memory skills. The important point really is to look at the details and, if you are only given a general IQ score, ask your educational psychologist for the breakdown of the subtests. This enables you to examine the above issues in terms of the child's actual cognitive profile and whether the IQ is a good reflection of that, as well as some of the issues about what it tells us in respect of underlying cognitive processes.

As the Wechsler and other individually given tests are closed and available only to educational or chartered psychologists, the teacher will need to choose some other tests of ability as a substitute.

NFER–Nelson produce a number of verbal reasoning tests, but of course the problem for dyslexic children is that these very often involve reading questions. As far as the verbal scale given above is concerned, I would suggest that the British Picture Vocabulary Scale (BPVS) is used.

The second edition looks at receptive or comprehension vocabulary in English and has an age range from 3 to 18 years. There are also alternative norms for pupils for whom English is not their mother tongue.

I would suggest that, as far as a Non-Verbal test is concerned, there are two possibilities. One is the Matrix Analogies Test (MAT) (Naglieri, 1985), which is a test of visuospatial reasoning. This involves various different forms, including pattern completion, and is very similar to the other test that I would recommend, which is the Raven's Matrices (see Appendix). This comes in two forms – one, standard, for a wide variety of age ranges, including adults, and the Coloured Raven's which is also a test of visuospatial reasoning for younger children. Additional measures of verbal ability might include the Mill Hill Vocabulary Scale or the Crichton Vocabulary Scale. All of the above are available from NFER–Nelson, apart from the MAT test which is available from the Psychological Corporation (see Appendix).

Teachers using these tests will be able to obtain a quotient or centile, which will give some general guide to overall ability. They will also be able to look at any discrepancies that there might be between verbal and non-verbal abilities, and form a basis for looking at the relationship between ability and reading and spelling levels. This can be done by developing a graphic display similar to that in Figure 3.1. Here we can include, for example, the BPVS and the Raven's Matrices scores expressed as quotients instead of the WISC scores, and instead of the Wechsler Objective Reading Dimensions (WORD) scores we can use other forms of reading and spelling tests. A further example of this is given later in the chapter (see page 42).

Attainment tests

We now turn to attainment tests, and in the case history given there are three taken from the WORD. These are the written language tests associated with the Wechsler scales. They are often used by educational psychologists because they enable one to produce a predicted standard score based on IQ. This in turn enables one to look at the statistically significant difference between the predicted score and that which is actually observed. In the case given, one can see that the predicted scores based on the Full-Scale IQ of 107 are around 104 or 105, depending on the particular attainment examined. The actual standard scores are also shown, which are lower at quotients of 76, 68 and 80, respectively. The differences between predicted and observed scores are statistically significant at the $p < 0.001$ level. Basically, this means that the differences between the observed and the expected reading scores are only likely to result from chance once in a 1000 times. This discrepancy analysis is, in my opinion, a crucial first stage in the identification of specific learning difficulties because it points to a specific underachievement. Other parts of the assessment are trying to tease out the cause of this particular under-achievement.

These are issues that are discussed by the recent British Psychological Society Working Party on the assessment of dyslexia, where there have been suggestions that this discrepancy analysis taking into account intelligence is not the most important facet of assessment. These are important issues which are taken up in Chapter 4 in some detail because it is an area of potential controversy, and it is important for the reader to understand the issues involved (as well as hearing my own particular view, of course!).

To return to the case, we have a discrepancy between the child's actual reading and spelling performance based on the standardization sample given in the WISC and WORD. More simply, we can look at the reading and spelling ages and note that the child's basic reading is some 3 years behind his chronological age. Basic Reading on the WORD is an individual word recognition test. Spelling is at least 4 years behind chronological age, and reading comprehension is 2.75 years behind. In the case of the WORD, Reading Comprehension is tested by the child reading short passages to himself or out loud, and then being asked questions about it, so there is some element of reading–decoding skill involved as well.

Further analysis of reading is given from the Neale Analysis of Reading Ability Test. Accuracy involves reading a series of graded passages and looking at the errors made. Comprehension is slightly different from the WORD in the sense that, if an accuracy error is made, the word is supplied to the child. Questions are asked at the end so that there is less of a word-decoding element. Finally, the Rate is simply the speed of reading.

Whatever reading tests are given, the first stage of the attainment process is to look at the general levels of performance and how these might relate to overall ability. Figure 3.2 shows how this can be done using the Matrices, British Picture Vocabulary Test (BPVS), the WRAT Reading (individual word decoding), Spelling and Arithmetic. It is taken from examples given at the Dyslexia Institute by Martin Turner. I have included this example because it illustrates some elements of the error of measurement that we discussed in Chapter 2. Rather than an individual point for the graph, as shown in Figure 3.2, you have what look like rectangular shapes. The top and bottom of each of these shapes represent the range or error of measurement for the particular test. Obviously, if there is a great deal of overlap between them, there is not much discrepancy between ability and attainment. On the other hand, if, as in the example showing BPVS/MAT and WRAT reading, there is little or no overlap, we can be pretty sure that there is a significant discrepancy between ability and attainment. This graphic representation is particularly useful because we do not have a statistical interpretation of the attainment/intelligence discrepancy as is given on the Wechsler scales, for example. It also enables a wide variety of different tests to be used in order to compare the child's attainments, (assuming they give standardised scores with a mean of 100).

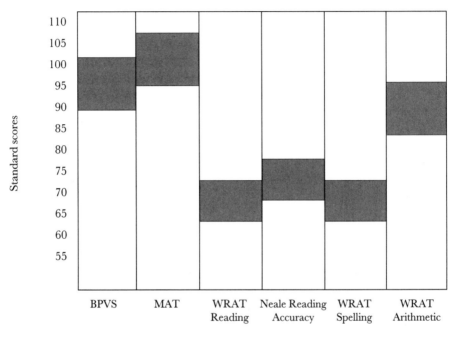

Test administered

All the above results, except for the MAT, are expressed at the 68% confidence level, i.e. one can be sure, about two-thirds of the time, that the subjects' 'perfect' or 'true' score would lie within the upper and lower limits indicated. The MAT gives confidence of 85%. The results above represent a graphical display of the table below.

Example: CA 8:4

Test	Raw score	Standard score	Standard error of measurement	Range	Confidence level (%)
BPVS	80	95	±6	89–101	68
MAT	27	101	±6	95–107	85
WRAT Reading	17	67	±5	62–72	68
Neale Reading Accuracy	12	72	+5	67–77	68
WRAT Spelling	12	67	+5	62–72	68
WRAT Arithmetic	21	90	+6	84–96	68

Figure 3.2 Graph showing standardized tests expressed in confidence bands. Reproduced with permission of Martin Turner, the Dyslexia Institute.

Of course, looking at a child's reading and spelling age and stating that there is a significant weakness is just the start of the story. This emphasizes the underachievement, and once again the reader is referred to Chapter 4 for details of the evaluation of this discrepancy exercise (see page 47). What is also equally important is to look at the reading and spelling errors and the way in which the child undertakes the reading process. Some examples of reading and spelling errors are given in the particular case history, and we can see problems of letter order, omissions of vowels, difficulties with end sounds, etc. A very important part of the diagnostic procedure is to write down errors and see how these relate to the way that the child operates in his reading or spelling task, e.g. *gup* for *jump* is a reasonable error because the child is using the 'g' as a soft 'g' for the 'j' in jump. On the other hand, he is omitting the nasal blend and we can relate that to some of the diagnostic tests that might be undertaken as well.

There are many other important aspects of looking at a child's reading performance, e.g. Where does a child start on the page? Does he need to follow a line when he is reading? Does he ignore punctuation? What is his knowledge about text in general? A detailed analysis of reading and spelling errors is of fundamental importance to plan help with reading and spelling. Of course, sometimes this is difficult to interpret, e.g. is *aminal* for *animal* a result of misreading caused by sequencing or 'jumping' of letters, or is it the result of the child recognizing the word correctly and mispronouncing the word *animal*? There are obviously basic factors to observe, such as difficulties with vowel combinations or consonant blends, but it is also worth looking in some detail or asking the children themselves, as well as listening to the way in which they go about reading and spelling to give clues about where the learning difficulty lies.

As well as formal reading and spelling tests, we also need some form of measure of writing. This can include free writing, where we are asking a child to write about anything he likes or to make up a story, or it might be more formal assessment in which, for example, we give 10 words and the child has to write 10 sentences using each word, and then we look at the writing rate.

It is often difficult to evaluate writing. We attempted to do it in the Aston Index (Newton and Thomson, 1976) by providing a series of categories such as grammar, writing style, etc., under which teachers could rate the child's performance. We need to just look at it qualitatively and make some comments as has been shown briefly in that case history. It will be seen a speed of six words per minute is given – there are norms produced by Hedderly (1995) which I find useful for this.

As far as attainments are concerned, teachers have a much wider variety of tests to choose from. The reader will have his or her own favourites, but I think there needs to be at least a word recognition test involving individual graded words, similarly with spelling, and at least a test involving the reading of text or some sort of comprehension. Individual word-reading tests include the Wechsler WORD Reading given above and the British Ability Scales Word Reading; Schonell is another one as is the Wide Range Achievement Test (WRAT). As far as reading from text is concerned, there are the Neale Analysis of Reading Ability, Individual Reading Analysis, the Salford Sentence Reading, and many others. In spelling there are the Vernon Spelling Test, British Ability Scales, WORD and WRAT tests. As far as writing is concerned, there is the Sentence Completion Test by Hedderly (see Hedderly, 1995). There are many other tests. Most of the above are available from NFER–Nelson or, in the case of the WRAT, from Wide Range in Delaware. (See the Appendix for the tests mentioned above.)

Diagnostic tests

Finally, we turn to diagnostic tests. Very broadly, these lie within two types, one of which includes diagnostic screening tests for dyslexia. As the purpose of these is to be a full assessment of them, it is not my purpose to review them here. They include the Bangor Dyslexia Test and the Aston Index, both available from Learning Development Aids (LDA) and both aimed at screening for dyslexia, and also the Dyslexia Screening Test produced by Fawcett and Nicholson (see Appendix), available from the Psychological Corporation. The second kind of diagnostic tests are those specifically trying to tap a particular element associated with specific learning difficulties or a particular aspect of reading, writing and spelling problems.

In our case history (see page 14) there are two tests quoted. One is the Phonological Abilities Battery and the other is the Non-Word Reading Test. The latter (Snowling, Stothard and Maclean, 1996) is, as the name suggests, a graded test of non-word reading, going from simple one-syllable words to two-syllable words with unusual letter–sound combinations. Non-word reading is proposed to be a measure of pure alphabetical skills or grapheme–phoneme correspondence skills, and it may be seen that our example has an equivalent age of 7 years on this particular test. This obviously indicates grapheme–phoneme correspondence difficulties, again common to many children with dyslexia. The other test, the Phonological Abilities Battery (Frederickson, Frith and Reason, 1997), indicates problems with both beginning and end deletion, i.e. the removal of a phoneme or a sound in a word, e.g. 'sand without 'n' becomes sad?'. As would be expected from the reading and spelling errors, this child has problems with both, but not with other elements of this particular test battery.

At this stage it is worth looking at elements of phonological skills because they are seen to be very important in the aetiology of dyslexia (see Chapter 9 for details). There are a number of tests that have tried to look at this. Table 3.2 gives some examples of how phonological skills could be examined. This shows four kinds of tasks. Under each of these four tasks are different levels. From (a) upwards the tasks become increasingly difficult. In other ways, I think the table is fairly self-explanatory.

Table 3.2 Examples of assessing phonological skills

1. Segmentation tasks	(a)	Counting syllables and phonemes. Tapping tasks (syllables or phonemes)
	(b)	Identifying syllables and phonemes, e.g. first part of 'carpet'
	(c)	Supplying missing syllables and phonemes, e.g. ca(t) or (c) at
2. Blending tasks	(a)	Blending syllables – car'pet
	(b)	Blending onset and rimes – c'at or tr'ip
	(c)	Blending phonemes – c'a't
	(d)	Single syllable and multi-syllable phoneme blending
	(e)	Non-word blending, e.g. v'u'm or t'e'k'o
3. Rhyming tasks	(a)	Rhyme detection, e.g. picking a word that rhymes with a picture
	(b)	Rhyme production – day, say, pay, jay, etc.
	(c)	Odd one out tasks – mad, cap, tap, sap
4. Manipulation tasks	(a)	Deleting phonemes – cat without (c) = at
	(b)	Adding phonemes – mee + t = meet
	(c)	Substituting - 'c' for 'p' in 'pat' to make 'cat'
	(d)	Transposing – John Lennon = Lohn Jennon

Adapted from Muter (1997) Paper at BDA Conference, York.

These and other approaches have, therefore, given rise to a number of tests that purport to measure phonological skills. Non-word reading, which attempts to measure alphabetical decoding without lexical (word meaning) knowledge, appears in the Phonological Abilities Battery and there is the NFER–Nelson Children's Test of Non-Word Repetition (Psychological Corporation), the Hatcher Sound Linkage Test of Phonological Awareness, the Posner Test of Auditory Analysis Skills, etc.

In addition to the above, there are a number of tests that also look at short-term memory skills, information-processing skills, etc. These include tests from the Aston Index such as the sound-blending, sound discrimination, auditory sequential memory and visual sequential memory tests, which are all linked to written language learning difficulties. Auditory short-term memory is also part of the WISC (Digit Span) and tests such as the Coding from the WISC can also be considered diagnostic.

The purpose of diagnostic tests is to delineate specific difficulties that the child has and link these to developmental remediation. This is beyond the scope of this book but see, for example, Thomson and Watkins (1999). The Dyslexia Institute also has a number of tests that it has developed for teachers, many of which are reported in *Dyslexia Review*, the journal of the Dyslexia Institute.

Further reading

The following give more detail on assessing the dyslexic child.

Miles TR (1993) *Dyslexia: The pattern of difficulties*. London: Whurr.
Reid G (1998) *Dyslexia: A practitioner's manual*. Chichester: Wiley, Chapters 3 and 4.
Thomson ME (1990) *Developmental Dyslexia*. London: Whurr, Chapter 5.
Thomson P, Gilchrist P (1997) *Dyslexia*. London: Chapman & Hall, Chapters 2 and 3.
Turner M. (1997) *Psychological Assessment of Dyslexia*. London: Whurr.

For more information of teaching, the following are useful (the second book mentioned also has a chapter on building a teaching programme from an assessment).

Thomson ME, Watkins EJ (1999) *Dyslexia: A teaching handbook*. London: Whurr.
Townend J, Turner M, eds (2000) *Dyslexia in Practice: A guide for teachers*. New York: Kluwer/Plenum.

CHAPTER 4

Definition and discrepancies

Introduction and context

There has been an increasing tendency over the last few years for a return to the notion of dyslexia as part of a general continuum of poor readers. In the 1970s, the thinking, particularly favoured by educational psychologists, was that dyslexic learning difficulties were a result of over-anxious parents or perhaps those 'middle-class parents with thick children'. In other words, that parents were reluctant to accept that their child was a slow learner, and used the word dyslexia to describe his or her difficulties. There were particularly hostile reactions from many in the educational world re the notion of a syndrome of dyslexia, and you can imagine the relief in dyslexia circles when specific learning difficulties/dyslexia was recognized by the 1982 and subsequent Education Acts.

However, there has been a suggestion of a return to the 'dyslexia does not exist' notion by some academics, e.g. Stanovich (1994), or 'dyslexics are just poor readers', e.g. the report of the working party of the Division of Educational and Child Psychology of the British Psychological Society. The following is their working definition of dyslexia:

> Dyslexia is evident when accurate and fluent word reading and/or spelling develops very incompletely or with great difficulty. This focuses on literacy learning at the 'word level', and implies that the problem is severe and persistent despite appropriate learning opportunities. It provides a basis for a staged process of assessment through teaching.

This definition has been rightly criticized by the British Dyslexia Association and others as being far too general, and might be applied to all children who are poor readers and spellers. However, the crucial element of this working party is the rejection of the notion of the relationship between reading (and written language) and intelligence as an important element of the diagnostic process in dyslexia. The notion of the discrepancy model in dyslexia has been questioned by some researchers such as Stanovich (1994), following on from Siegal (1989) as well as this working party. There are very important implications for diagnosis, policy and remediation from these questions, which have been fuelled in particular by the idea that there is a core phonological deficit, which is the descriptive definition of dyslexia, and not a discrepancy between observed reading, writing and spelling and that expected based on intelligence and chronological age.

This is ironic, considering the history of the concept of dyslexia and its interrelationship with educational psychology theory and practice. In the early 1970s, dyslexia was described as essentially a syndrome by identifying particular features that were associated with dyslexia, e.g. see Miles (1974) and Newton (1970). These features included weak auditory and visual short-term memory (particularly sequencing), but also sound blending, sound discrimination, naming and labelling skills, all of which have been described as being associated with a phonological deficit in more recent years (see also Chapter 1).

The idea of describing a particular learning difficulty in terms of its observed deficits was rejected by the educational psychology establishment at that time. However, the key epidemiological studies, e.g. Rutter et al. (1970) and Yule et al. (1974), established 'specific reading difficulties' and dyslexia became accepted. This was on the basis of the proposal by Yule et al. (1974) that there were groups of children who could be divided into those who had general reading retardation and those who had a specific reading retardation. This was on the basis of the relationship between IQ and reading. There was found to be a high correlation (around 0.6) between reading and intelligence, and Yule et al. were able to demonstrate that children whose reading was 2 or more years behind their chronological age alone showed a different pattern of learning difficulties from those children whose reading was 2 or more years behind that based on chronological age *and* intelligence. (See Chapter 1, page 5, for a summary of the differences and for further details.) Taking into account the notion that reading is not perfectly correlated with intelligence, they developed regression equations – which enabled them to predict what reading should be in a given population – early on in the Isle of Wight and later in the Inner London Education Authority, based on four subtests of the WISC, giving a short-form IQ, and using the Neale Analysis of Reading Ability.

This study was widely accepted as 'proving' that there was indeed a dyslexia syndrome, and this was based on the discrepancy model very widely accepted by educational psychologists since then. Over the last few years there have been criticisms of both a technical and a theoretical nature (see Thomson, 1990, for a review). However, it is ironic that the Division of Education and Child Psychology is now rejecting the notion of a discrepancy model in favour of describing various characteristics of the learning process (mainly involving phonological skills) that describe dyslexia, when it was educational psychologists who rejected characteristic descriptions in favour of discrepancy models.

IQ/reading relationships

The critical examination of this relationship by Stanovich (1994) is based on points made by Siegal (1989). She argues that intelligence tests do not truly measure intelligence, and that some of the items measured by such tests are, in effect, measures of achievement, not of intelligence. The implication is that an intelligence test needs to have predictive and concurrent validity, i.e. it correlates with future academic performance and current achievements. Well-validated tests such as the WISC do this, and to argue about the construct of intelligence and what the tests measure is rather sterile. Concerns over the construct of intelligence and what items should be included in intelligence testing do not, it seems to me, preclude examining the relationship between reading ability, for example, and an intelligence test score. Of course, it is the case that children who are, as she put it, 'from minority backgrounds, lower social class families and/or different ethnic groups' may be disadvantaged, but essentially an IQ score is useful for its guide to what a child might do at school later on, and in defining certain cognitive skills. This still seems to be a valid construct if we look at the standardization manuals for both British Ability Scales and the Wechsler scales. Of course, we must be careful not to label as slow learners those children who are not; this is part of the educational psychologist's training and clinical experience, although this does not mean to say that we can use the recognized impreciseness of psychometric testing to throw out the concept altogether.

Siegal also goes on to comment that 'calculating a discrepancy . . . seems an illogical way of calculating whether or not there is a learning disability'. I would argue to the contrary, because it is quite clear that it is possible to examine the relationship between intelligence, however imprecisely measured, and reading (also, it should be noted, imprecisely measured as reading involves many different kinds of skills and most reading tests measure these only inaccurately). The Yule and Rutter studies demonstrated how it was possible in a given population to look specifically at the relationship between attainment and IQ skills (or, if arguing about the constructs, Wechsler IQ scores and Neale Analysis of Reading Scores), whatever they measure. The most recent additions to the British

Ability Scales and the Wechsler scales include discrepancy tables that have been standardized on US and British samples (and in other countries where the scales are used). The data from these large samples are sufficient evidence that there is a relationship between attainment tests and IQ. Table 4.1 shows examples of the predicted attainments based on full scale IQ on the WISC-III and Wechsler Objective Reading Dimensions (WORD). It shows that, for a given IQ, on the left, we can predict the quotient on Basic Reading, Spelling and Reading Comprehension following on from the standardization samples in the Wechsler scales, in this case the British sample. One should also note that this takes into account the so-called regression to the mean effect, which has also been a criticism about attainment/IQ discrepancy analysis. In other words, the correlation between reading and intelligence as measured by intelligence tests is not perfect. There is a regression to a mean, i.e. children with lower IQs will tend to have higher predicted scores for attainments, and children with higher IQs will tend to have lower predicted scores for their attainments. This deals with the statistical criticisms concerning IQ/reading correlations. Note that regression to the mean is not the same as the regression equations used to predict reading level from age and IQ. Table 4.1 illustrates how the regression to the mean occurs based on predictions of attainments from IQ in the standardization.

Table 4.1 Predicted WORD attainments for WISC IQ

Full-Scale IQ	Predicted attainments		
	Basic Reading	Spelling	Reading Comprehension
75	85	87	83
105	103	103	103
125	115	113	117

We can now look at some specific examples of how this discrepancy can be analysed using recent psychometrics. The tests shown below also enable us to see whether differences in profile are the result of chance variation or statistically significant differences.

Table 4.2 gives typical examples of a current method of examining the difference between predicted reading quotients and observed (actual) attainments. From this, the traditionally 'discrepant model' child with dyslexia, case 1, is over 3 years behind chronological age in reading, but the difference between predicted reading and observed reading quotients is also significant at the $p < 0.001$ level. (The difference is statistically likely to be caused by chance only 1 in 1000 times.).

Table 4.2 Predicted reading quotients, based on Full-Scale WISC-III IQ and observed reading quotients

---

'Dyslexic child', IQ 107, CA 10;5

Predicted reading quotient	Observed reading quotient	Difference	Statistically significant
101	70	31	$p < 0.001$
10:9	6:6		
53rd centile	2nd centile		

'Slow learning child', IQ 77, CA 11:5

Predicted reading quotient	Observed reading quotient	Difference	Statistically non-significant
86	91	5	
9:3	9:6		
18th centile	27th centile		

'Slower learning and dyslexic child', IQ 82, CA 9;11

Predicted reading quotient	Observed reading quotient	Difference	Statistically significant
89	63	26	$p < 0.01$
8:9	6:0		
23rd centile	1st centile		

'Bright dyslexic child', IQ 120, CA 10;7

Predicted reading quotient	Observed reading quotient	Difference	Statistically significant
112	88	24	$p < 0.01$
13:9	9:0		
79th centile	21st centile		

This sort of analysis indicates that it is quite possible to look at the relationship between attainment and intelligence in a statistically and conceptually valid manner, despite Siegal's contention that it is illogical. It is interesting to note that the dyslexic child above would fall at the 2nd centile, which is the (arbitrary) cut-off point used by many local authorities to provide full-time specialist support for children with specific learning difficulties. The 'slow learning' child (case 2) – or certainly the child who does less well on intelligence tests, whatever that might mean conceptually and operationally – has an expected reading level broadly within the average range (between the 25th and 75th centiles), even though his reading skills are weak and some 2 years behind chronological age.

The final argument that Siegal puts forward and which Stanovich, in particular, has taken up, is that poor readers with average or higher IQs are no different from poor readers with lower IQs. I do not think that anyone who is working seriously in the area of dyslexia has ever argued that all dyslexic children are intelligent. However most teachers argue that there is a great deal of difference between teaching a child who is a poor reader due to low ability and a dyslexic child.

A key feature in defining dyslexia is to examine those particular aspects of the child's learning difficulties and skills that are independent of intelligence, or at least the results of the IQ produced by an intelligence test. Simply, this means that there are just as likely to be dyslexic children who score less well on IQ tests as those who score very well on IQ tests. Intelligence would be just one aspect of a child's psychometric profile. The 'slow learning dyslexic child' (case 3) shown in Table 4.2 illustrates this point. Here, we have an individual who does less well on IQ tests, but his reading is still well below that based on the prediction on both IQ and chronological age. So, we can see an individual with lowish IQ who, even with discrepancy analysis, we would describe as dyslexic. Of course, no one would pretend that just the discrepancy analysis on its own is a sufficient reason for describing an individual as dyslexic – we have to look at a whole number of other factors discussed in Chapter 3.

It is of interest to note in passing, before we go on to examine this issue further, that Stanovich (1994) himself proposes a kind of discrepancy notion in his identification of 'dyslexia'. This is that there should be a discrepancy between decoding in reading comprehension. This is less practical and begs a lot more questions than the IQ/reading discrepancy. The reason for this is that most comprehension tests in reading rely on word reading, e.g. in the Neale Analysis the reading test is discontinued once a certain level of Accuracy has been reached. Furthermore, on this particular test if a child makes an Accuracy error, whether it is mispronunciation or anything else, the correct word is supplied. On the other hand, in the WORD Reading Comprehension, the test involves reading a passage silently (or aloud) and then answering questions. No corrections are given, and the comprehension score is quite clearly linked to reading decoding or accuracy. Other tests include 'cloze' procedures, sentence completion tasks, etc. There is therefore a great deal of variety in what different reading comprehension tests actually measure; in most they are heavily loaded and correlated with reading decoding skills. Furthermore, unlike the IQ/reading dimensions, we do not have standardization correlations or predictions for comprehension/decoding. If 'verbal comprehension' is used, i.e. oral comprehension as has also been suggested, then this is an intelligence test item, is it not?

The notion of a core phonological deficit

We now turn to the idea of a core phonological deficit being the main descriptor and, by implication, identifier of dyslexia. The BPS Division of Educational and Child Psychology (1999), following Stanovich and others, argues that we should be looking at core phonological processing difficulties as the main diagnostic criteria for dyslexia. These include problems with naming, sound patterns, phonemic awareness including segmentation, whether it be at phoneme, onset/rime or syllable level, phonological recoding, i.e. grapheme–phoneme correspondence, etc. There is a great deal of research indicating that these and other skills, such as early rhyming abilities, are good predictors of later reading and spelling development in the normal population, and are often weak in children with reading and spelling difficulties. We examine these in Chapter 9. Stanovich and others who wish to do away with the intelligence/reading dimension propose that we should be examining this as a fundamental description of 'dyslexia'. The notion here is that children of both high and low IQ would show core phonological deficits. Unfortunately this proposal does not quite hold up. Frith (1999) makes the point that low 'g' or general intelligence can underlie the behavioural weaknesses in children with dyslexia, i.e. weak non-word reading, phonemic awareness problems, slow naming speed in tests as well as difficulties with reading and spelling. Coltheart and Jackson (1998) make this point particularly well in talking about proximal and distal causes, which I have adapted and presented in relation to this issue in Figure 4.1. Here we have similar behaviour with different aetiologies.

As Figure 4.1 shows, the cause of a phonological deficit can be the result of a number of different factors. These are the 'distal' causes. The phonological deficit itself is the proximal cause (e.g. of reading difficulty). One distal cause can be low intelligence or, if you prefer, low scores on an

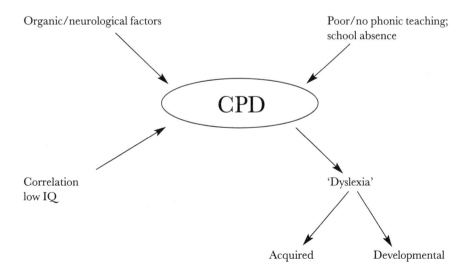

Figure 4.1 Different 'causes' of a core phonological deficit (CPD).

IQ test. The evidence is that intelligence test scores, as one measure of 'g' or underlying intelligence, are correlated with many different academic achievements in all walks of life and particularly at school age. Therefore weak phonological skills could be caused by low IQ, some neurological or organic difficulty, but also, crucially, it can be the result of lack of teaching, poor phonic teaching at school or even school absence. Weakness in core phonological skills can give rise to dyslexia, whether acquired or developmental. The reason (distal cause) is the observed phonological difficulty (proximal cause).

Now, it can be argued that it could be core phonological problems in both children with dyslexia and those who are slow learners that cause reading difficulties, but I would suggest that the different aetiologies of these are crucial in terms of the teaching programme that is undertaken. This differential teaching has been one of the main reasons for identifying individuals with a dyslexic problem as opposed to general learning difficulties. This has given rise to all the teaching programmes that are specifically used for children with dyslexia (see Thomson and Watkins, 1999, for examples). Furthermore, when we look at the reality of assessing children, it is quite common in my experience for dyslexic children to show phonological deficits (despite their high intelligence or scores on IQ tests), and for children who are slow learners or do less well on IQ tests to do quite well on phonological skills even though their reading is weak. In the case histories given (see Table 4.2), the 11-year-old described as a slow learner in fact had a Graded Non-Word Reading Test score (one widely agreed measure of alphabetical–grapheme–phoneme correspondence skills) at just under the 50th centile, whereas the dyslexic child had a score at around the 10th centile.

In addition, the whole notion of just phonological deficits as descriptors of dyslexia does not take into account many of the other problems that dyslexic children have in aspects of short-term memory, which are not specifically linked to phonemic awareness, in weak organizational skills, in arithmetic and tables skills, and in a whole variety of patterns of behaviour commonly recognized by teachers of dyslexic children.

The above should give plenty of food for thought for the reader; however, is it just me being cynical by saying that doing away with discrepancy notions means that fewer 'children with dyslexia' are identified if we ignore children who are of high intelligence? Examining the centiles and discrepancies of the 'bright' dyslexic child in Table 4.2, we can see that there is a discrepancy between the predicted and observed reading ages. However, because the child's centiles are still at a relatively high level and the child is only a year or so behind chronological age in reading, he would not be given any additional support. This is typical, in

my experience, of a number of children attending my school whose difficulties are not recognized as being severe by the local authority because
intelligence is not taken into account. Only those children who fall below
the 1st or 2nd centile in absolute terms are deemed to be severely
dyslexic. This saves resources, but is hardly reason enough to reject a
useful concept. Of course, no one should diagnose dyslexia just on the
basis of a discrepancy – it is identifying a problem. The next question is
the best estimate of what caused the problem.

Further reading

BPS (1999). Working Party of Division of Educational and Child Psychology. *Dyslexia, Literacy
    and Psychological Assessment*. Leicester: BPS.
Thomson ME (1990). *Developmental Dyslexia*. London: Whurr, Chapter 1.
Turner M (1997). *Psychological Assessment of Dyslexia*. London, Whurr.

Some of this chapter appeared as an article in *Dyslexia Review* **11**(4).

CHAPTER 5

Basic neuropsychology

As we see when we look at proposed causes of dyslexia, a number of theories focus on the neurology or neuropsychology of written language processing, where there are seen to be variations or 'deficits'. I have always viewed explanations for dyslexic difficulties at a number of levels. As far back as the 1970s (e.g. Thomson, 1977, 1979), I was arguing that there was a neurological and cognitive level of explanation and that dyslexia was an individual difference in learning style. The neurological differences would result in cognitive differences, which would in turn result in specific skills that were weak in people with dyslexia which then interacted with the written language system. In other words, we can examine what procedures are needed to learn reading, writing and spelling, how they develop and how they match with what an individual child might have.

These concepts are expressed more elegantly nowadays by, for example, Uta Frith (e.g. Frith, 1999), who talks about the biological, the cognitive and the behavioural level. An example of this general approach is given in Figure 5.1. These and further figures are a development of the outline given in the Preface. Readers may like to refresh their memory about the concepts briefly discussed there.

Here, the notion is that a developmental disorder has a primary biological cause. This might be genetic, which in turn might be to do with brain function or neurology. There is then a resulting cognitive deficit, and finally behavioural signs and observations that can be made. Interacting with all of this is the environment, which would be aspects of received teaching, experiences at home, other difficulties, psychosocial problems, etc., which might affect a child's learning and hence the behavioural observations, i.e. reading and spelling difficulties that might be seen.

We go into more detail in later chapters, examining different models of such a general causal framework and examining in detail the neuropsychological deficits, phonological coding deficits, cerebellar problems, etc.

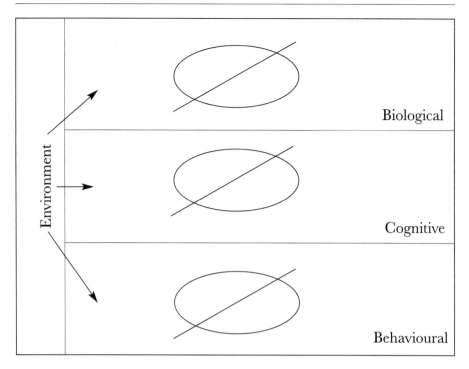

Figure 5.1 Deficit model: general causal model of neurocognitive origin. From Frith (1999) Paradoxes in Developmental Dyslexia, John Wiley and Sons. Reproduced with permission.

The reader should not forget that dyslexia is a disorder of written language. We look at models of how written language develops in children and what its characteristics are in Chapter 8. As I have argued elsewhere (Thomson, 1990), we need to look at the task demands of the written language system and see whether the skills possessed by an individual child match those task demands. The purpose of this chapter is, very briefly, to outline some key elements of brain function that we need to know before we examine specific theories of how brain organization might result in dyslexic difficulties.

Although the reader should not look upon this as a potted version of the biological basis of psychology, it does provide an overview of areas of the brain and sensory function that are relevant to dyslexia. These are picked up later in Chapters 6 and 7.

Brain function and anatomy

In general terms, we might describe the relevant aspects of neuropsychology that we wish to consider as (1) the sensory/perceptual and (2) the linguistic/cognitive. The sensory/perceptual domain includes the sensory pathways, i.e. the sense organs, the eye and ear being the most obvious and important ones in the case of reading and spelling, although of course motor function is also important. As well as sensory pathways, this would include aspects of the brain stem, i.e. the underlying, older parts of the brain which undertake a number of functions. This includes the cerebellum, which we examine in more detail in a later chapter. Also important are 'relays', including the thalamic relays where information is passed on from the sensory organs to the brain. An example is shown later in the visual system in particular. The sensory/perceptual information that comes from our sense organs goes to various parts of the cerebral cortex. The cerebral cortices are the higher centres of brain function. Those associated with receiving information from the senses are called the primary cortices, including the primary visual and the primary auditory cortex (situated in the occipital and temporal lobes, respectively). Finally, we could include the association areas of the brain as important elements of the sensory/perceptual function. Perception, as opposed to sensory input, implies that the brain is to some extent constructing a model of the world, but that is perhaps taking us into other realms of psychology.

The so-called linguistic/cognitive approaches are much more to do with higher-order functions. Those parts of the brain responsible for language are particularly important when it comes to dyslexia, as we see later (page 61). These include part of the cerebral hemispheres – involving the anterior temporal cortex, inferior parietal lobes and frontal lobes. Before we look at some of these functions, a brief simplified overview of brain anatomy is required.

Figure 5.2 shows a very crude model looking at the four major lobes of the brain from the left point of view. Note that the dotted lines are arbitrary.

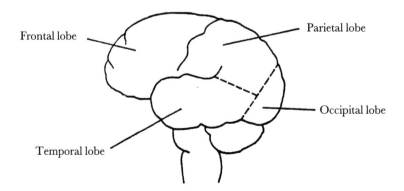

Figure 5.2 Major lobes of the cerebral cortex.

Figure 5.3 shows examples of the relationship between the cerebrum in humans and some examples of the brain-stem structures such as the mid-brain, hindbrain, cerebrum, cerebellum and spinal cord. The functions of these are outlined in Table 5.1.

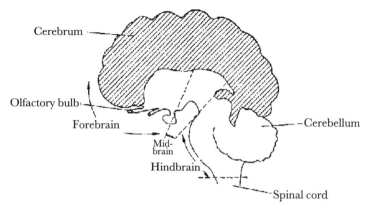

Figure 5.3 Cerebrum and brain stem.

Table 5.1 Parts of the brain and their associated language functions

Cortex: concerned with the receipt and recognition of others' speech, as well as the formulation, initiation and control of own

Cortical lobes with speech areas	All the lobes are important in the speech processes since any sensory impulse may make connection with the speech association areas .

Subcortical structures: concerned with the organization and relay of sensory and motor impulses to and from the cortex

Basal ganglia	Involved in the control of the muscles of the face, larynx, tongue and pharynx. Damage to them may lead to lack of coordination in articulation, gesture and facial expression.
Thalamus	Organizes and relays sensory data on the way to the cortex. Sensory concepts, which affect speech, may be organized here, as well as the emotional qualities of the voice.
Midbrain	On the sensory side it contains relay stations concerned with sight and hearing. Similarly, on the motor side, it carries the pyramidal and extrapyramidal tracts.
Medulla oblongata	Contains motor nuclei for controlling basic body functions, such as breathing, together with the motor and sensory tracts connecting with the midbrain.
Cerebellum	The control centre for continuous muscular movements and coordination. Damage to it results in speech which is jerky, thick and slurred.

Figure 5.4 shows a diagram of the left hemisphere with various language functions highlighted. Some descriptions of the functions are also given.

Note, especially for Figure 5.4, that these areas do not have exact delineations in brain matter. Although there is obviously agreement as to location, different books have different style diagrams and the labelled sites indicative of general areas.

There now follows some additional comment on some of the key areas from Figure 5.4. The auditory association area has obvious implications for spoken to written language, but note the description of the planum temporale (temporal planc) because we shall be looking at anatomical differences between children with and those without dyslexia in this area in our later discussions on causes.

Broca's area is also important, because there is an integration here between the production of speech sounds, which is important in early articulation difficulties, phonemic awareness and the relationship

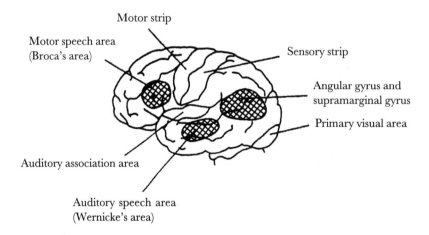

Figure 5.4 Left cortical hemisphere showing language areas. These are: auditory association areas (first temporal convolution): this area is essential for the recognition and analysis of spoken language. This area lies adjacent to the 'planum temporale'. Wernicke's area lies between this and the angular gyrus.
Broca's area and lies just anterior to the motor area that controls movements of the face and mouth, is essential for the production of coordinated speech sound.
Motor strip for writing and articulation.
Supramarginal gyrus: within this area the sounds of the words become associated with their meaning.
Angular gyrus: within this area, the patterns of written symbols become associated with their verbal counterpart and with the concept they represent.

between phonological knowledge and later reading, writing and spelling. These are key skills, as we shall see our later descriptions of the reading and spelling processes, and we also re-examine these concepts in terms of cerebellar and other theories of dyslexia.

The angular gyrus is also of particular interest. One of the earlier notions of dyslexia used to be the concept of 'soft neurological signs' or 'minimal neurological dysfunction', and typically the description of Gerstmann's syndrome was used here. This was a syndrome involving four key difficulties: loss of written language, acalculia, left/right discrimination and finger agnosia. These problems were suggestive for individuals with dyslexia, although the finger agnosia perhaps was not so commonly observed. 'Finger agnosia' is based on a test where the subject closes his or her eyes and two fingers are touched by the examiner. The subject has to decide which the two fingers are, and those with finger agnosia find this difficult.

Cerebral dominance and bilateral function

The parts of the brain described above are important for dyslexia but also important is the notion of 'cerebral dominance'. The cerebral cortex, as is widely known, is split into two halves – not totally because there are connections between the two lobes – but these are differential functions. The left cerebral hemisphere, for most people, is responsible for language functions, but also serial order, sequencing, and coding sorts of tasks. The right hemisphere, on the other hand, has greater facility with three-dimensional, spatial or 'gestalt' kinds of task.

The notion of a dominant hemisphere refers to the idea that spoken language is one of the 'higher-order' or evolutionarily more sophisticated skills, and therefore the hemisphere that is primarily responsible for this kind of task is the 'dominant' one. The term was coined by early neurologists who observed how damage to various parts of the brain gave rise to particular difficulties. The notions of how the cerebral cortices are organized for this language dominance has important implications for dyslexia. We examine this in detail in Chapter 6.

Moving to a consideration of some of the sense organs and the way in which information comes into the brain, it is worth looking at some examples of the sensory perceptual pathways, in particular examining the way in which sensory and motor mechanisms are crossed, because these have implications for cerebral dominance. If we look at the motor and sensory paths concerning handedness, a topic we also consider later (see page 73), we can see that these are completely crossed. This is shown in Figure 5.5.

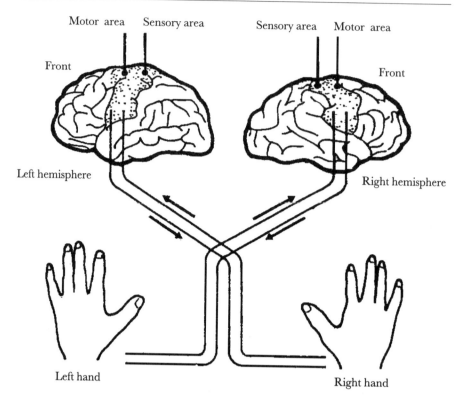

Figure 5.5 Motor and sensory pathways to the hands.

Thus, if there is damage to the motor area connected to the hands on the right hemisphere, the ability to use the left hand is lost. Similarly, if there is a stroke in the language functions of the left hemisphere, particularly Broca's area, there would tend to be loss of motor function in relation to speech. This is well known to most readers.

There is also some information on the visual route to the cerebral cortex. This is important for another reason – to illustrate the fact that the visual system is not as simply contralateral as the motor and sensory systems of, for example, a hand or foot. Basically this means that information coming into the left visual field is dealt with in the right side of the brain and information coming into the right visual field is dealt with in the left side of the brain. This is found from studies using tachistoscopes, i.e. information is presented on a screen for varying lengths of time and subjects are required to fixate on a central point. Linguistic information, including letters, words, numbers and stimuli requiring a name code, that is presented in the right visual field is perceived or remembered or dealt with cognitively much more easily than linguistic material presented in the left visual field. This would imply a left hemisphere that is better at language processing and a right hemisphere processing that is less efficient for language-based materials.

Conversely, visuospatial material, e.g. shapes, figure representations, etc., that is presented in the left visual field is dealt with more easily than that presented in the right visual field, again giving evidence for this notion of the right hemisphere being spatial rather than linguistic. The visual field is quite complicated in the sense that there are various different relay bodies. Figure 5.6 shows how visual information passes from the visual fields to the optic chiasma where the inputs are divided. Left visual field input goes to the right hemisphere (dotted line) via the lateral geniculate body, and vice versa (solid line).

There are also crossover points where information is transferred from the right to the left hemispheres. It is obviously not the case that we process

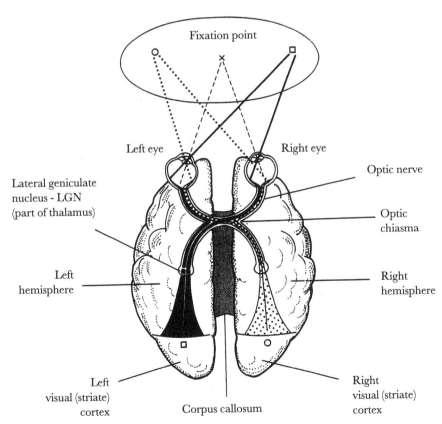

Figure 5.6 Input of visual system to cerebral cortex.

information only from one side of our visual field in each side of the brain, although that is where the information goes first. What happens then is that information is transferred from one side of the brain to the other via a structure called the corpus callosum (see Figure 5.6). The same thing happens, of course, for other sensory and motor functions.

There has been some very interesting work on what happens when people have had the corpus callosum severed. This used to be the treatment for some severe epilepsies and often people might, for example, be able to hold an object in their left hand and explain what it was used for, but not give it a name. This was because the information about the object being held in the left hand was transferred to the right hemisphere and the access point for the name of the object, which was located in the left hemisphere, e.g. supramarginal gyrus (see Figure 5.4), could not be accessed because the information was not transferred across by the corpus callosum.

Interesting work has also been done on 'divided visual field studies', where people with dyslexia are asked to look at information in left and right visual fields and the implications that might have for cerebral function, which we look at later.

The notion of the left hemisphere being responsible for serial order and symbolic skills is, of course, very interesting to those theorists who were trying to look at the written language system that appeared to be serial order, temporal and symbolic kind of functioning. The notion of two sides of the brain undertaking two different functions interested researchers as far back as the 1930s, when they were trying to develop theories about dyslexia, and we examine some of the more modern theories later.

The examination of the visual system is also important, because we shall be looking not only at theories of cerebral dominance, but also at some specific theories on the visual deficits in dyslexia, particularly the visual transient system and others in which we will need to know a little about the visual system and cerebral cortex structures.

The auditory system also has complicated contralateral connections, although it is not as complicated as the visual system in terms of its laterality and crossover. It may be seen from Figure 5.7 that the auditory pathways are partially crossed. Each hemisphere can receive input from both ears, but the neural collections from one ear to the hemisphere on the opposite side are stronger than the connections to the hemisphere on the same side. In the figure, the cochlear nucleus is part of the auditory input

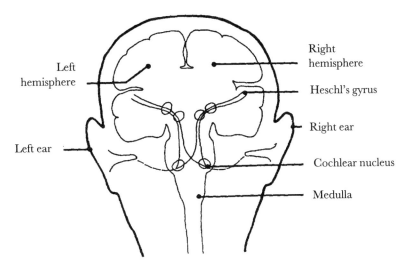

Figure 5.7 Contralateral connections in the auditory system.

relay system, as is Heschl's gyrus. The medulla is simply the lower brain-stem part of the midbrain.

The sort of model of brain function in terms of auditory input that has been built up is based on research such as dichotic listening, e.g. auditory material that could be words, numbers, music or other acoustic phenomena is presented to both ears at the same time. If the information is verbal, such as numbers or words, individuals report or deal with or remember that information presented to the right ear rather better. This, of course, implies left hemisphere processing because there are stronger contralateral connections (from the right ear) to the left hemisphere. On the other hand, if the information is less verbal, more melodic, etc., it is much more likely to be better perceived in the left ear, although there is not quite such clear-cut evidence for this.

These sort of neurocognitive studies, such as studies of divided visual fields and dichotic listening, were cognitive psychologists' approaches to build on the early neurologists' mapping of the cerebral hemisphere system, which is based on language in the left hemisphere and non-language or three-dimensional skills in the right. These, of course, were described by the early neurologists who observed what happened in brain-damaged individuals. Thus, if a particular part of the left hemisphere had been damaged, language functions would be lost, whereas damage to the same part of the right hemisphere would not result in language loss in an individual.

When we look at causes in Chapter 6, the reader may just need to refresh his or her memory on some of these basic concepts, and we examine them in the context of explanations for dyslexic difficulties.

Further reading

Any psychology text, for example:

Atkinson RL, Atkinson RC, Smith EE, Bem D (1993). *Introductions to Psychology*. Orlando, FL: Harcourt Brace Jovanovich, Chapter 2.
Gross R (1992). *Psychology: The Science of Mind and Behaviour*. London: Hodder & Stoughton, Chapters 4 and 8.

More specifically on written language:

Ellis AW, Young A (1988). *Human Cognitive Neuropsychology*. Barringstone: Lawrence Erlbaum.
Robertson J (2000). *Dyslexia and Reading: A neuropsychological approach*. London: Whurr, Chapters 1 and 2.

CHAPTER 6

Neuropsychology of dyslexia

This chapter examines and focuses on the biological basis of dyslexia. The assumption here is that dyslexia has a neurocognitive origin, as illustrated in Figure 5.1 (page 57).

It may be seen from this figure that, at the biological level, there is some kind of 'brain abnormality'. This in turn gives rise to cognitive deficits and the behavioural signs. (These are also discussed in the Preface.) Of course the environment impinges on these and this would include appropriate teaching, adaptation to learning difficulties, etc. This is an important point to make at this stage, because it is very easy to assume that a cause of neurological origin means that nothing can be done to help the child. This is akin to going back to the old notion of 'word blindness' as a description of dyslexia. The reality is that we are looking at an individual difference. This may be the result of the way in which the brain is organized and processes the information, but I personally do not like the use of the term 'abnormality' or 'deficit' in searching for neurological explanations. We might just as well invent notions of 'dysgolfia' to describe individuals who seem congenitally unable to hit a golf ball correctly or straight (I include myself in this syndrome). The individual difference here is that my brain is not organised very well to strike a golf ball. We can easily examine and analyse the skills required, e.g. visual focus on the ball, smooth draw back of club, timing, etc. We could then look at the particular part of the brain that undertakes these skills, finding that my brain does not have the processing skills to deal with one or more elements that I need to strike the ball, and therefore I have an 'abnormality' or a 'deficit'. However, just as I can be taught how to play golf reasonably well despite a brain not tuned to it, so we can teach a child with dyslexia to read and spell!

Before we look at brain function, however, we need to look at genetics because the implication of a biological basis is for a genetic predisposition.

Genetic factors

It has been recognized for some time that dyslexia 'runs in families'. At East Court we often find that fathers, mothers, siblings and other members of a family may also have dyslexia problems to a lesser or greater degree. To reiterate my above comments, it is worth noting that a genetic predisposition does not imply that nothing can be done to help a child with dyslexia. Dyslexic children (or adults) can learn to read fluently and spell competently. The key is to present the written language system in a way so as to meet their way of processing information.

One of the first studies in genetics was by Hallgren (1950). He believed that dyslexia was determined by an alternative form of gene, placed on a chromosome other than a sex chromosome. He drew the conclusion that the data he had obtained best fitted an autosomal dominant genetic mechanism. However, since then there have been many researchers who have criticized Hallgren's method of analysis and questioned his conclusions. Stevenson et al. (1987) noted that he made no attempt to distinguish between specific and general retardation, and used language and speech delays as evidence of reading problems. It was also found that Hallgren used reports of the child's difficulties rather than an actual assessment of their performance. The concept of a non-sex-linked difficulty has also been challenged, because it appeared that a greater number of males than females were affected. It was suggested that the gene could be dominant in males, although recessive in females (Sladen, 1971; Finucci et al., 1976). However, a high incidence of reading disabilities in a family may not be a sufficient indication of genetic transmission. There could be other causes of the effect, such as shared environment, particularly the educational environment created by parents for their children.

Later studies looked in more detail at the familial incidence of dyslexia. Owen et al. (1971) found reading difficulties in children to be particularly associated with fathers. This might have been socially determined (e.g. modelling on a parent), but it was also found that there were neurological immaturities present in both siblings (a dyslexic child and his or her sibling) that cannot be learned socially, e.g. problems were found with reproducing auditory tapped patterns, distinguishing double simultaneous touch, carrying out fast alternating finger and hand movements, and making right and left discriminations. If these problems are present in siblings it is thought to be an indication of underlying mechanisms that are acting on both children. As these aspects are not socially controlled a familial incidence would not be related to the environment. Similar results to these were found in the Colorado Family Reading Study (1973, cited in DeFries and Decker, 1982) when whole families of probands were compared with those of control families. The greatest difference between the families was found to be that of their reading abilities, with all members of proband families performing significantly more poorly than those of the control families.

It is possible to apply Waddington's (1957) theory of canalization to the findings for dyslexia, as argued by Owen et al. (1971). According to this theory, the developing phenotype can be represented by a ball that rolls through valleys of varying widths and depths. At some points, a deflection can send the phenotype into different channels of development whereas, at other points, a major deflection is required to change the course because the genetic canalization is very strong. In relation to dyslexia this means that the impact of genetics can be stronger for different aspects of the disorder. The deep canalizations represent strong genetic influence and it takes a lot of environmental pressure to alter the phenotype from this point. However, when the genetic effects are weaker and the channels not so deep, the environment can effect behaviour relatively easily.

It could be the case that certain types of dyslexia are transmitted genetically, and that this may occur through multifactorial inheritance (Owen, 1979). This means that the disability may be determined by a number of genes, each of which contributes a small amount to the whole trait. The extent and expression of these genes in terms of phenotype would be a function of an interaction of a genetic predisposition, environmental experiences and changes in the effectiveness of the methods of treatment used.

Linkage studies

Linkage studies work on the basis that, if a trait can be shown to be linked to a known genetic marker locus, then it can be inferred that a major gene for that trait is located on the same chromosome as the marker locus. Smith et al. (1982) looked expressly at families in which a specific reading disability appeared to be inherited through several generations in an autosomal dominant manner. There was found to be a link between specific reading disability and chromosome 15. The effects of genetics can be studied by looking at families, comparing the siblings and parents of children with dyslexia with those of non-dyslexic children, as was done in the studies of Hallgren (1950) and Owen et al. (1971). Another way of looking at genetics is to examine twins and how alike their reading patterns are. Studies conducted using this method examined both monozygotic and dizygotic twins, and these were separated into those raised together and those raised apart.

Twin studies

The basis of twin studies is the difference between monozygotic (MZ) and dizygotic (DZ) twin pairs, based on their genetics. MZ twins have identical genes, whereas DZ twins have, on average, half of the same genes, i.e. as any other sibling. It is assumed that DZ twins are brought up to share the environment to the same extent as MZ twins. This means that, if there is any greater similarity between an MZ than a DZ pair, this must reflect genetic influences. In terms of dyslexia, if both twins are affected, they are known as concordant; if not then they are discordant. A greater MZ than DZ concordance provides evidence for a genetic aetiology.

Before 1987, Bakwin (1973) collected the largest quantity of data about twins and reading disabilities. He identified 338 twin pairs, of whom 97 children displayed difficulties with reading. Pairwise concordance was found to be 83% for MZ twins and 52% for DZ pairs. Many criticisms were aimed at these earlier studies, particularly in view of the discrepancy between the results obtained.

Stevenson et al. (1987) found that, when IQ was controlled for, spelling heritability was 73%. However, concordance rates for reading backwardness and specific reading retardation were found to be low in both MZ and DZ twins; the concordance was found only for spelling difficulties. They accounted for the differences between these findings and those of previous researchers by the fact that the previous studies had not used a truly representative twin sample. They also believed that there could have been an age effect; they looked at twins who were 13 years old, whereas the other studies had tended to focus on children at younger ages. They argued that genetic influences might not be as pronounced at the age of 13 as they were in younger children. Nevertheless, the apparent genetic influence on spelling disabilities seems to be more prevalent than that of the other areas.

The Colorado twin study was perhaps one of the more noteworthy studies conducted on twins with regard to reading problems (DeFries, 1985, 1991). The results of this study were that, proband-wise, concordance rates were 70% for MZ pairs and 48% for DZ pairs. This led DeFries to conclude that there must be at least some genetic aetiology for reading disability. Further analysis using multiple regression estimated that about half of the deficit found in probands was the result of heritable influences. When Olson et al. (cited in DeFries, Gillis and Wadsworth, 1990) looked at different areas of reading, they found that the link between word recognition and phonological coding was significantly greater than that between word recognition and orthographic coding.

They took this to mean that the genetic aetiology of deficits in word recognition may have been caused by the heritable influences on phonological coding.

The specific mechanism of genetic predisposition may be linked to phonological coding skills, in terms of the human genome and particular chromosomes and linkage methods that were reviewed above.

Using previous evidence of genetic studies of dyslexia, Pennington (1999) started with the idea that it must be genetically heterogenous and that it was likely that more than one gene was involved. He thought that possibly all reading ability is influenced by a number of genes, and that dyslexia is just one variation of these genes. He also pointed out that the locus for dyslexia is not disease, but susceptibility. A susceptibility locus, unlike a disease locus, is neither necessary nor sufficient to produce the disorder. This would explain why there does not always appear to be a genetic link, and why some children who are expected to have inherited dyslexia do not meet the criteria. If a susceptibility locus influences a continuous trait, it is called a quantitative trait locus (QTL). There are usually several QTLs required to influence a complex behavioural trait such as dyslexia.

If a small number of QTLs underlie the transmission, then traditional linkage analysis may not be applicable. In Pennington's (1999) study he used sibling pair linkage analysis. He found evidence for a QTL on the short arm of chromosome 6; this evidence was consistent across two independent samples of sibling pairs, two sets of genetic markers and different researchers (Cardon et al., 1994; Grigorenko et al. 1997; Fisher et al., 1999; Gayan et al., 1999). Grigorenko et al. (1997) also found linkage for a different phenotype, that of deficits in word recognition, with a marker on chromosome 15. This repeats the findings of Smith et al. (1982); there was thought to be a double dissociation between the genes influencing the two phenotypes. This led to the view that QTLs are genes that somehow lead to disruption in epigenesis and development, which in turn may eventually alter learning to read. However, the studies of Fisher et al. (1999) and Gayan et al. (1999) both found that deficits in phonological and orthographic coding were related to the same region of chromosome 6.

The above review is only a sample of some of the work on dyslexia and genetics and, although the reader may feel that it is already too technical, it can get much more so! The general conclusion we need to take away is that there is a genetic vulnerability to dyslexia in some individuals. According to Pennington, if one parent is dyslexic, 50% of the children inherit this vulnerability and 100% of children inherit if both parents are dyslexic. Note the word vulnerability; this implies that educational and environmental input can prevent reading and spelling failure. Let us move on to how a genetic predisposition might affect brain function.

Cerebral dominance and dyslexia

We examined notions of cerebral dominance in the human brain in general in Chapter 5, and it is particularly on this area that a good deal of research in dyslexia has focused.

The notion of a human brain that is mainly left hemisphere dominant for language, serial order and sequential skills, with the right hemisphere responsible for three-dimensional skills, has implications for dyslexic children. The former constitutes the tasks with which they have difficulty and the latter, in terms of observations of people with dyslexia who do well at three-dimensional spatial tasks, seems to be the task at they do well.

The first person to try to relate the idea of dominant hemisphere function to dyslexia was Orton (1937). Without going into detail on his theory, he proposed that words and letters were stored as the mirror image of what was seen in the opposite hemisphere, e.g. the word 'saw' was stored as 'saw' in the left hemisphere but as 'was' in the right hemisphere. This resulted in reversal and mirror imaging and the other features he observed in many people with dyslexia. The notion of mirror-image storing of 'engrams', and his rather simplistic theory of the wrong hemisphere being accessed by mistake, has since been superseded, but he was the first to draw attention to the notion that there could be some element involved.

A number of theories have proposed a relationship between cerebral dominance and dyslexia. These are presented in Table 6.1, along with my comments in the right-hand column. The detailed evidence of all of these is reviewed elsewhere (Thomson, 1990), but it is worth examining some of these issues as an historical perspective.

Table 6.1 Theories of aetiology relating to cerebral hemispheres

Lack of cerebral dominance. No left hemisphere dominance, or less clear cut	Some evidence but different interpretations of data possible
Maturational lag or delay in left hemisphere language processing	Would expect adults to show no deficit, but they do. Some evidence, however
Left hemisphere deficit of some kind	Some evidence
Interference by right hemisphere. Right hand favoured	Too complex, not parsimonious
Disassociation of auditory and visual material in different hemispheres	Some evidence

In the UK, Newton (1970) proposed a lack of dominance in people with dyslexia. Her early work involved the examination of electroencephalographs (EEGs), using resting records. An EEG is a measure of the electrical activity that occurs in the brain. It is measured by sticking electrodes on to people's scalp and observing what happens by means of a printout of 'brain waves'. There are various rhythms that are produced when we are alert and conscious, when in sleep, dream, etc. Early work at the University of Aston examined alpha rhythms in dyslexic and non-dyslexic children. Alpha rhythm (6–10 cycles per second) occurs when people are awake in a resting state with eyes closed. It was found that the alpha rhythm from the angular gyrus region in particular (See Chapter 5 for the importance to written language) was symmetrical in children with dyslexia, i.e. there was an equal amount of alpha rhythm from both hemispheres, whereas in control children there was much more alpha rhythm activity in the left hemisphere.

Also, at around this time, the notion of inconsistent laterality was put forward as evidence for a lack of dominance. As seen from our examination of the way in which our brain and brain sensory motor systems are set up, there are contralateral connections between the sides of the brain and the opposite sides of the body. This has led a number of individuals to comment on the higher incidence of left-handedness and ambidexterity among dyslexic individuals. This was an important feature of my early work on people with dyslexia (Thomson, 1975). A lot of recent work on laterality has suggested that it is largely inherited; there are some interesting theories on the way in which mixed handedness might also be better for three-dimensional skills and less good for verbal and written language skills (see Annett, 1991).

In my experience this tends to be very much a probabilistic observation (see Thomson, 1975, for a Bayesian statistics, a probability analysis). There are dyslexic children who are right-handed or right dominant, and there are a number of children who are not dyslexic and who are left-handed or mixed dominant. However, there seems to be a higher incidence of one than the other. This is illustrated in Table 6.2 taken from clinical studies of over 500 children at the University of Aston. Here, handedness is compared between people with dyslexia and the general population.

Table 6.2 Handedness in dyslexia children and the general population

	Right-handed	Mixed-handed	Left-handed
General population	68	28	4
Dyslexic children	20	67	13

(University of Aston)

Sometimes the relationship between laterality and dyslexia (i.e. more mixed handers) is found in populations of children referred to clinics, whereas it is not found in general populations, when looking at overall poor reading. This, I think, results in some of the conflicting evidence and a detailed discussion is given in Thomson (1990). This relationship has not examined the concepts of cross-laterality, e.g. children who are left-eye dominant and right-handed who may have difficulty in scanning and sequencing, but is included here to provide an historical context for the development of a neuropsychological picture of dyslexia.

Moving on from laterality, at around this time, other evidence began to support the notion of a lack of hemisphere dominance, particularly in the dichotic listening and divided visual field studies.

In dichotic listening, the reader will remember auditory material presented to both ears at the same time. A typical result is given in Table 6.3 from my own studies (Thomson, 1976). Here, 10-year-old children, both dyslexic and non-dyslexic, were presented with numbers to the left and right ears. Table 6.3 shows the percentage of correct responses.

Table 6.3 Percentages of correct right ear recall in children with dyslexia and controls

	Children with dyslexia	Non-dyslexic children
Right ear	68	82
Left ear	65	68

The point of this table is to illustrate some of the problems with interpretation of data. Initially I interpreted the findings as suggesting a less clear-cut hemisphere dominance for children with dyslexia, i.e. when comparing the left and right ears in both groups, the control group children, who are good readers, show the normal right ear effect (REA). This implies better left-hemisphere processing for verbal material, in this case numbers. Children with dyslexia do not show this better performance in the right ear, i.e. no REA, and therefore one interpretation is that they do not have dominance of function for the left hemisphere. Both hemispheres perform equally at the same level. However, there is another interpretation of these data (can you suggest one without reading further?). I came to this following a discussion with Colin Wilsher, one of the research associates at Aston. If we compare children with dyslexia and controls among themselves, looking at the right ear alone rather than looking at REA, we see that children with dyslexia do less well. Therefore, the apparent lack of dominance may simply be the result of the fact that they are not as good on the right ear, i.e. there is a left-hemisphere 'deficit' of some kind. When we use indirect measures such as dichotic listening it is often difficult to come to absolute conclusions. There was a plethora of research in this area during the late 1970s and early 1980s, with people reporting different results and/or different interpretations.

The same thing happened in divided visual field studies (see Chapter 5 for details) where we are looking at the right and left-visual fields. I undertook a study with Graham Beamont and Michael Rugg (Beaumont, Thomson and Rugg, 1981), well-known researchers in the area of hemisphere function, which could be interpreted as suggesting that the children with dyslexia had a normal left-hemisphere function for auditory material (they did better for auditory material on the right ear, i.e. the REA). On the other hand, they were better on the right hemisphere for visual information (they did better in the left-visual field for shapes, etc.). This was not particularly conclusive because other findings contradicted this research, and indeed the notion of children with dyslexia doing as well as controls in auditory tasks in dichotic listening had not been found in some of my own earlier research.

Fortunately, later research techniques have thrown more light on the situation, suggesting both processing and anatomical differences in the way in which children with dyslexia deal with written language information.

As well as the resting EEG record, another common technique is the evoked response. An evoked response is looking at how a particular part of the brain responds to stimuli, e.g. in the visual evoked response, a strobe light flashes at, say, once per second. Electrodes are stuck on different parts of the scalp to measure activity from different parts of the brain (the way in which these electrodes are placed is based on an internationally agreed code to reflect parts of the brain). Initially, the EEGs show no reaction because there is random background activity. However, the records are passed through a 'computer of average transience', which averages out all the background activity; gradually this builds up a response to the strobe light in that particular part of the brain that is being recorded. This can also be done with auditory evoked responses using a sound and we can look at different stimuli – words, music, shapes, etc. A typical example of this, adapted from Connors (Connors, 1970; Connors et al., 1984), is shown in Figure 6.1. Interestingly, this shows both a child of 11 with dyslexia and a father and mother, aged 37 and 36, respectively.

The evoked responses are taken from the occipital and parietal lobes. It may be seen that the third curve (from the left parietal lobe) is what is known as 'attenuated', i.e. there is a reduced evoked response (in the Index, i.e. case of dyslexic boy, none at all!). This occurs both in the dyslexic child and to a lesser extent in the mother. This shows evidence, incidentally, of some genetic predisposition that was discussed earlier (see

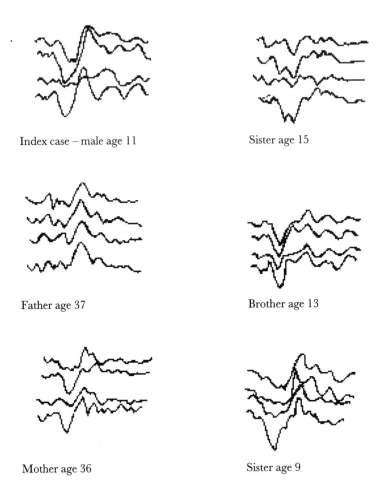

Index case – male age 11   Sister age 15

Father age 37   Brother age 13

Mother age 36   Sister age 9

Figure 6.1 Visual evoked potentials derived from left and right occipital and left and right parietal regions (10–20 system) in a family of dyslexic children.
Curves (top to bottom) are: left occipital, right occipital, left parietal and right parietal. Note the attenuation (weaker) of the left parietal tracing ms for all siblings. Adapted from Connors (1970), Connors et al (1984).

page 68); more important is the notion that there is no evoked response in a dyslexic child in a particular area of the brain crucial for language function.

Even research such as the above was not entirely without debate, resulting, possibly, from misinterpretations. However, one important aspect is that clinic samples, i.e. children referred to hospital clinics, generally in the USA, often show different patterns to children across wider populations, suggesting that there might be some other underlying neurological problem with children, in addition to the dyslexia, which resulted in referral, typically, to a neuropsychology unit, for such research to be undertaken.

However, further supportive evidence of the notion of left hemisphere differences continued with Galaburda's (1989, 1999) and Galaburda et al., (1985) anatomical studies. A typical example is given in Figure 6.2 which shows a horizontal cross-section of two brains.

As we saw when examining brain functions (see Chapter 5), the planum temporale (PT or temporal plane) is a very important area for language functions, particularly implicating sound and phonological processing, because there are close connections between this area and the primary auditory cortex. This provides us with a link between neuropsychology and the phonological coding and short-term memory weaknesses that people with dyslexia show (see Chapter 9).

Figure 6.2 shows that, in the control brain (rather morbidly taken from people with dyslexia *post mortem* – there have been an increasing number of people with dyslexia who have donated their brains after death to neuropsychology research teams), the PT is larger on the left hemisphere. The dyslexic individual, however, has a symmetrical PT, which provides direct anatomical evidence for a difference in hemisphere organization between people with dyslexia and control subjects.

The notion of a macroscopic cortical 'abnormality' (i.e. the anatomical differences) is matched by deeper explanations at the microscopic level.

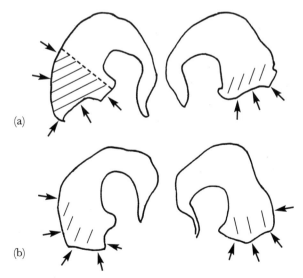

(a)

(b)

Figure 6.2 Cross-section of the temporal plane in a person with dyslexia and a control. Superior temporal plane in (a) a control brain and (b) the brain of a person with dyslexia. The extent of the temporal plane is indicated by arrows. The dyslexic brain has an almost symmetrical plane (flat upper surfaces of the temporal lobe). Adapted from Galaburda (1989, 1999)

One of the things that happens when the young fetal brain is developing is that cells migrate or move to different parts of the body, where they begin to take up their specialized functions. This happens with brain cells and is known as neuronal migration (brain cell = neuron). According to Galaburda and others, it is possible that, at around week 24 of gestation, when the cerebral cortex forms most rapidly, cortical ectopias (warts that are 1 mm in size) can develop. Neurons migrate past the outer membranes of the developing brain to form these growths, particularly in the parietal lobes of the left hemisphere. These have been observed in people with dyslexia in some of these anatomical studies.

Therefore, there could be problems in the developing fetus that give rise to 'deficits' in the left hemisphere, which are linked to aspects of language function and, by inference, written language functions; they are also linked to anatomical differences that may affect the way in which the brain is organized.

One final set of 'evidence' to round off our picture is the increasing use of magnetic resonance imaging (MRI). This is a technique in which pictures of the brain are taken when the individual is doing certain tasks, which could include verbal reasoning, reading, looking at shapes, jigsaw puzzles, etc. When the brain is doing these tasks it calls on further oxygen. This oxygen in the blood, which goes to the active brain area, shows up differentially on imaging techniques, usually as different colours or different intensities. A number of recent studies are indicative. In one (Shaywitz et al., 1998), the route that information appears to take when reading is from the primary visual cortex to the visual association areas (the angular gyrus), where words and letters are linked to language, and then the temporal gyrus (i.e. Wernicke's area) where the sounds of language are translated into words or some form of semantic access. This was the 'normal' route. However, in people with dyslexia, the final path was to Broca's area, where speech is processed, rather than to Wernicke's area; this suggests that there may be a problem with lexical access, i.e. finding names of words.

Paulesu et al. (1996) gave people with dyslexia rhyming and verbal short-term memory tasks; there appeared to be a weak activation of the pathways that carry information from Broca's area to the superior temporal area. This also suggests a problem with translating unsegmented into segmented speech. The segmentation, or the splitting of speech sounds into individual words, is a key feature of the phonological difficulties besetting many people with dyslexia (see Chapters 8 and 9). They concluded that only a subset of brain regions normally involved in phonological processing was activated. They further concluded that the 'neuropsychological and the PET findings both point to a disconnection between different phonological codes' (Paulesu et al., 1996, p. 154). This conclusion was reached because of the isolated activation of Broca's area, Wernicke's area and the supramarginal gyrus in the dyslexic subjects during the phonological tasks. Paulesu et al. proposed that such a disconnection can account for the difficulty experienced by dyslexic children in learning to read, and they suggested that, in learning to speak, children learn that the speech they hear maps on to the utterances that they produce. This mapping depends on connectivity between the relevant language areas in the brain. A weak connection would not only cause delays in this hearing–speech mapping, but will also cause difficulties in learning an alphabetical code that depends on mapping of graphemes, phonemes and whole word spelling and sound. Other research also suggests that the wrong information is transmitted to the parietal lobe because of the difficulties in tracking, but we look at this in more detail when we examine visual transient systems (see later).

So what are we to make of all this? In general, it seems that many areas of the left hemisphere may be implicated, but the puzzle is how these language areas can be affected so specifically. In other words, why are vocabulary, verbal reasoning and other higher-order language tasks robust, but written language is weak? Apart from very specific speech-to-alphabet skills, spoken language is also robust. As previously remarked I think that we should view dyslexia as an individual difference. The evidence suggests that there is an individual difference in the way that the brains of dyslexic individuals are organized that predisposes them to being rather better at three-dimensional spatial skills and creativity but less good at language skills, particularly those involving written language. Research seems to suggest that there may be a less clear-cut dominance of function for language tasks in general, but specifically for those written language tasks that involved elements of phonological coding and aspects of the phonological loop in working memory (see Chapter 9).

The most powerful evidence comes from MRI studies, and it is here that we begin to see a relationship between what is going on at the brain level and what we observe at a cognitive and, therefore, behavioural level. The brain of a person with dyslexia is less efficient at guiding aspects of speech processing, linked to phonological and grapheme processing, to the parts of the brain that are best at processing it. Bear in mind that this is relative. So, as we have discussed, people with dyslexia communicate and function normally in everyday life, by and large. It is when we force the brain to use processes and skills linked to other tasks, e.g. speech, sequential memory or temporal tracking, and apply them to written language, that we begin to see a 'system breakdown'. Our brain systems are geared up for communication, thinking and language, which are skills needed for survival, not reading. We invented written language and make our brains use systems that were evolved for other functions in order to learn to read and spell as children. Furthermore, it is only now, in the last 100 years, that reading and spelling have become a 'survival' skill for life – not surprising that some of us do not have brains as efficient for written language as they might be.

Further models of neuropsychological aetiology

In this section we consider some alternative hypotheses in relation to the causes of dyslexia. Phonological decoding and working memory problems have become central in aetiology (see Chapter 9), with the assumption that these follow from neuropsychological predispositions. However, there are many different approaches, some of which focus on the wider range of difficulties presented by people with dyslexia. As we have seen, dyslexia as a syndrome is not just simply about reading; it includes many different elements. In particular we consider two of the most well-formulated alternative theories – a cerebellum difficulty and a problem in visual processing system.

Cerebellar difficulties

Figure 6.3 is the familiar model used by Frith (1992) and looks at the various levels of explanation – biological, cognitive and behavioural – with input from the environment. In this case the model is used to reflect a cerebellar processing abnormality. The behavioural observations shown here, such as poor naming speed, poor time estimation, poor motor development and balance, are obviously particularly linked to this theory. A cerebellar abnormality is also linked to timing and sequential deficits which, it is argued, can lead to phonological problems, as shown in Figure 6.3.

We can look in more detail at this approach mainly as a result of the work of Nicholson and Fawcett (1999). They draw attention to the role of the cerebellum in a number of verbal tasks. They argue that a significant part of the brain is often overlooked as a result of the emphasis on cortical hemisphere function. The cerebellum (see Figure 5.3 in Chapter 5) is mainly a motor area involved with balance and initial motor skills learning. It is the area that is involved with enabling motor skills to become automatic, i.e. to be developed without any conscious thought or analysis. A good example might be learning to ride a bike or perhaps a game such as squash. Initially when we learn such tasks, we have to pay attention to what we are doing. Often coaching emphasizes thinking about how – for example, in squash – the racquet is held, how the arm is moved, the position of the body, etc. As this task becomes automated or 'over-learned' we

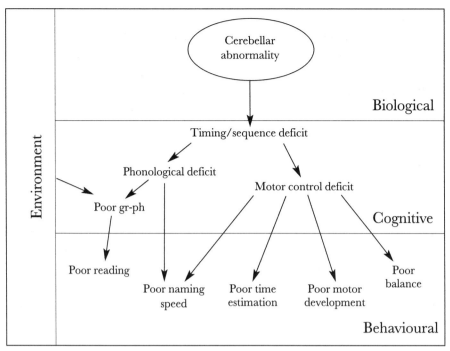

Figure 6.3 Causal model as a result of cerebellar processing abnormality. From Frith (1999)
Paradoxes in Developmental Dyslexia, John Wiley and Sons. Reprinted with permission.
gr-ph ≡ grapheme-phoneme correspondence

can undertake the same movement again and again without thinking
about it. However, as well as motor skills learning, the cerebellum has a
role in the automation of other cognitive skills. In particular there are
neurological links to the cortex, including Broca's area (see Chapter 5),
which is involved in aspects of language dexterity.

It is argued that the cerebellum has a role in developing language,
particularly the development of articulatory skills, where the cerebellum
seems to be involved in timing and fluency. We can therefore imagine
how easy it is to make the connection between articulation and phonological awareness, a link that has often been made by those who propose a
phonological deficit for people with dyslexia. However, the cerebellum
will also account for problems with spelling and handwriting. Disorders
of the cerebellum can give rise to difficulties in posture and muscle tone
(dystonia), and problems with posture or movement of the extremities
(ataxia).

In addition to these observed features, the impairment of the cerebellum gives rise to difficulties in automisation of skills and, in particular,
immediate recognition of letters and spelling patterns. Skill performance
or motor tasks rely on the expectation of smoother performance as they

are 'over-learnt' or automated, and require less effort after practice. Those of us who observe children struggling to learn to spell can see this lack of automation. Sometimes a dyslexic child may spell correctly and sometimes he or she will make a mistake. The skill of spelling has not been automated in the sense of being smooth or quick, or requiring less effort with practice!

Nicolson and Fawcett (1999) have undertaken a considerable amount of research in this area, looking at both gross and fine motor skills. They found, for example, that people with dyslexia asked to do a balancing task were as good as control individuals when just simply doing the task on its own, but, if they had to undertake a dual balancing task, i.e. do a secondary task involving, for example, counting, they were weaker. Similarly, using reading age controls they found that a wider variety of tasks were weaker in people with dyslexia. These included not only spelling, segmentation and picture naming, but also balancing and bead threading. They argue that it is both phonological and motor skills that are affected, particularly involving automisation and information-processing speed. It is interesting to note that the latter is a key psychometric weakness as well (see Chapter 3).

Nicolson and Fawcett developed some screening tests as a result of their theoretical formulation, the Dyslexia Screening Test (DST – see Appendix), and Figure 6.4 presents a summary of the approach (Nicolson and Fawcett, 1999).

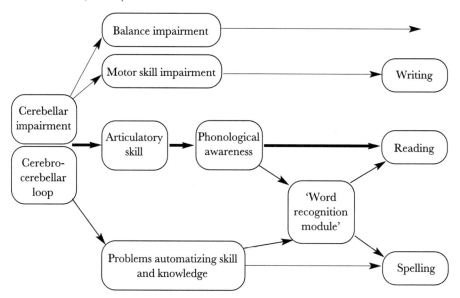

Figure 6.4 Proposed causal chain for the cerebellum and reading. From Nicolson and Fawcett (1999) Developmental Dyslexia: The role of the cerebellum. John Wiley and Sons. Reproduced with permission.

In Figure 6.4, the right-hand side shows writing, reading and spelling. This model accounts for weaknesses in phonological awareness – (see Chapters 8 and 9) – but it also accounts for problems in automating skills and knowledge. It is the automisation that introduces a new element to the learning process, and links motor skills and skilled task learning in general to reading and spelling.

In this model, phonemic awareness difficulties result from problems in articulatory skill, which in turn come from impairment of the cerebellum, not on its own, but crucially the link between the cerebellum and the cerebral cortex. Therefore, we have a fairly formalized theory trying to account for the overall reading problems of people with dyslexia, both phonological difficulties and other areas of weakness such as reading, writing and spelling. One criticism of the theory is the question: why are there some people with dyslexia who do not appear to show motor deficiencies? I have known many children with severe dyslexia who are gifted 'sportschildren' and whose motor skills, balance and coordination are exceptionally good. On the other hand, quite a few children with dyslexia have overlapping difficulties in what we might call 'dyspraxia'. In general, this can refer to motor skills and movement or, in verbal dyspraxia, articulation or language problems (or both!). At my own school, for example, we can observe a number of difficulties in these areas.

The following is an extract from a description given by Sue Flory, the specialist 'motor development' teacher at East Court:

> He will lack coordination to such an extent that, even when walking, will give the appearance of being held together loosely with string. He will bump into furniture and people. This is because he lacks awareness of his own body and himself in space; he may not receive the information he needs from the environment around him through his senses, and, if he does, he may not be able to interpret, order and use it. He will fall over and fall off his chair more often; and fidget and be unable to stay still like other pupils. He may lack control in the use of his voice, speak too loudly, interrupt and have unusual intonation and breathing patterns when talking. Games and playground play are difficult; because he does not have the skill and coordination to join in successfully, he invades others' space and touches too heavily because he has not the muscular control or feedback (the problem is compounded if this is perceived by others as aggression).
>
> Organization of himself and his belongings is a constant problem, particularly if he has to move around school from class to class. Things are forgotten or dropped, and progress is slow. He usually looks untidy, shirt out, socks on inside-out, shoes undone, even on the wrong feet; trousers can occasionally be on inside-out or back to front! Food is invariably down his front and all around his mouth.

The 'skills learning approach' has personal resonance for me. When I was doing my doctorate way back in the 1970s, I was taking the view that we should look on language learning as a skills-based system. It made a lot of sense to look at reading, writing and spelling in terms of skills analysis, and subsequently to look at the kinds of task demands made by the system in terms of what a young child needed in order to meet the requirements of that task. Written language is an artificial system, and what we are trying to do is use a series of cognitive and other systems that we happen to have in our 'learning armoury', in order to learn a task that we are not evolutionarily prepared for. We are geared up for spoken language, but devised the written language as a second symbol system.

Visual difficulties

The next alternative theory is the role of the visual system. It has been received wisdom that people with dyslexia do not have difficulty with seeing as such, i.e. although some might complain that the letters jump around or that they lose their place, the problem is not in the primary visual system. It is assumed that any difficulty connected with the visual system is at the level of perception, i.e. how the brain builds up a picture of the world.

It would, however, be foolish not to comment on the primary role of eyes in relation to receiving information from the world and, in particular, reading. There has been a good deal of work showing that people with dyslexia have erratic eye movements. I have reviewed this work in some detail elsewhere (Thomson, 1990), but some of it is worth reiterating. Figure 6.5 shows examples of typical eye movement patterns of a person with dyslexia. The first part (a) of Figure 6.5 shows the typical saccadic movement that results when a fluent reader is reading text, i.e. the eyes move across the page in a series of saccades or sweeps, fixating on a word, then moving on. The labels are fairly self-explanatory and the bottom part of the figure (c) shows the typical saccadic pattern on a different scale. The other two examples (b) are from dyslexics (Pavlides, 1981). We can see how erratic these are, involving, as they do, moving backward and forward over the page, regressive eye movements and disordered movement.

Most psychologists believe that erratic eye movements are a secondary factor in dyslexics, i.e. they are a result of dyslexia and not its cause. This is a good example of the interrelationship between reading and proposed cause. On page 124, we discuss the role of appropriate research groups in dyslexia, and here is an illustrative example. The eye movements are the result of the difficulty of that test for that individual, e.g. a fluent reader might be presented with an obscure legal text, which is usually dense and difficult for the non-lawyer to understand. Here, the reader's eye movements might well be erratic with a regressive pattern and eyes going back to check over the text to try to make sense of it. It may be re-read again and again. There might also be attentional focus difficulties! This is not because the reader has dyslexia, but because of the difficulty of the text. Thus, if you

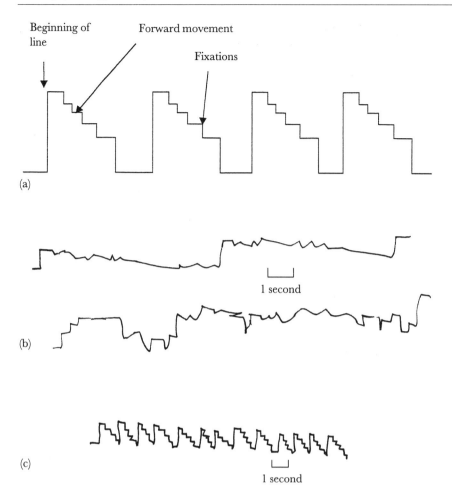

Figure 6.5 Normal and erratic eye movements. (a, c) Typical saccadic movement when fluent reader is reading text. (b) Saccadic patterns of two people with dyslexia. From Thomson (1990) after Pavlides (1981).

take a 10-year-old child who is dyslexic and perhaps reading at the 6- or 7-year-old level, and give him a text with a reading level of 10 years, he will find this difficult. Any erratic eye movements are a result of the difficulty of the text, not of some primary eye movement problem. In other words, as you learn to read, so your eye movements become more fluent, particularly when you are reading a text that is easier than your reading level. Therefore, erratic eye movements simply say that the reader is having difficulty with the text that he or she reading – it is an effect not a cause.

There have, however, been some more recent approaches looking at the role of the visual system, particularly associated with the work of Stein (e.g. Stein and Talcott, 1999). Essentially this revolves around speed of processing, especially the rapid processing of visual events, including reading. In particular, the focus is on rapid visual processing via the magno-cellular pathway. Here, readers might remind themselves of the visual path-ways coming into the brain, as shown in Figure 5.7 (Chapter 5).

Figure 6.6 shows a causal model of dyslexia as a result of the magnocel-lular abnormality in the biological, cognitive and behavioural terminology used by Frith. In Figure 6.6, we can see that the core difficulty is with slow temporal processing. We can now look at the route that visual information takes when going into the cortex, as demonstrated in Figure 6.7.

The first visual input is obviously via the eye to the retina. In the retina there are cells known as the magnoganglion cells, which have fast links to the lateral geniculate nucleus in the thalamus. From the thalamus, there are routes via the deep magnocellular structures to the primary visual cortex. This is the part of the cerebral hemispheres that deals with visual information. It is here that integration with other signals and visual processing occurs, which include a number of different aspects, but particularly the following two:

1. What kind of patterns, shapes and forms are seen in the environment (this includes elements of visual acuity and structure)?
2. Where?

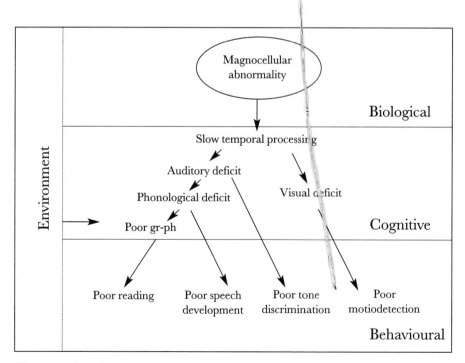

Figure 6.6 Causal model: a result of magnocellular abnormality. From Frith (1999) Para-doxes in Developmental Dyslexia, John Wiley and Sons. Reproduced with permission. gr-ph ≡ grapheme-phoneme correspondence

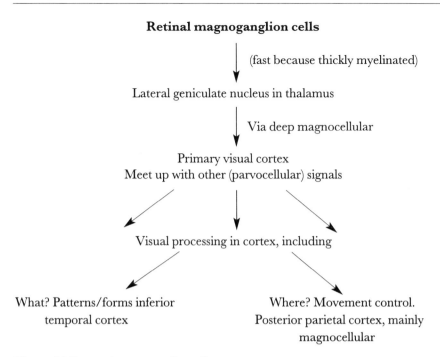

Figure 6.7 Route of magnoganglion cells to cortex.

Visual processing at this point involves particular elements of movement control. As seen from Figure 6.7, the processing occurs in different parts of what is the temporal cortex. Movement control is in the posterior parietal cortex where magnocellular structures are located.

The magnocellular cortex consists of large neurons which process transient, i.e. moving, visual and auditory information. The cells in the optic pathways are split into large and small retinal ganglion cells. The large cells – around 10% – are magnocellular cells and the smaller ones are parvocellular structures. Table 6.4 summarizes the difference between the two types of cell.

Table 6.4 Magno- and parvocellular differences

Magnocellular	Parvocellular
Visual transience	Sustained response
Illumination change	Continued focus
Movement including flicker	Static displays
Low light and contrast	Colour
Moving targets	Visual acuity (detail)
Fast conduction	
Eye movements	
Binocular control scanning	
Temporal sequence	

Eye movements, binocular control scanning and temporal sequence are crucial elements of the visual transient theories of dyslexia.

Having described the various pathways and briefly the anatomical and functional aspects of the magnocellular system (MCS), we now turn to how it affects reading. Basically, the MCS guides the eyes to the target. Eye movements take place in a series of flicks to the target and, in the case of reading, this gives us the step-wise saccadic movement shown earlier, which is important for developing stable fixations on points to which the eyes move, but it also gives rise to an effect called suppression. This essentially enables us to move our eyes from position to position or to track objects without any blurring of what we are looking at. In other words, our eyes move, not the world. As well as movement, which primarily involves following a reading target as you move across it, the MCS is involved in vergence eye movement (VEM). VEM, as the name suggests, is to do with the mechanism that results in our two eyes focusing and converging on a particular target. Some of the early work of Stein and Fowler (1985) suggested that people with dyslexia had binocular instability, which resulted in difficulties in fixation, but particularly the relationship between tracking a text and fixating a target. Quite clearly if you are unable to track a target or fixate on the orthography, i.e. a particular letter combination at which you are looking, there will be a problem in phoneme–grapheme mapping. Thus, phonemic awareness and grapheme–phoneme mapping skills, which are described as a phonological disorder in people with dyslexia, could equally be the result of a problem in visual fixation of the orthography, as opposed to the relationship between speech-processing systems and phonological representations.

In reading, the MSC also guides the fine detail of the saccades or movement sweeps, e.g. the saccade has 30 milliseconds of movement with a 250-millisecond fixation on average. If we look at the normal eye movement in reading, there are about three letters before and five letters after the central fixation point that are taken in, in a given 'visual chunk' as it were. If we look at the following example:

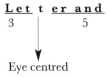

According to research by Stein, people with dyslexia are impaired by flickering stimuli and have problems with low contrast flicker and motion. However, they are normal or perhaps better at colour and fine detail (see comments on page 87). According to Stein, there is also some evidence that the MSC is smaller and disordered in dyslexics, and he and his colleagues draw attention to the importance of the interrelationship of temporal scanning, visual transience systems, binocular controls and all of these elements in relation to letter–sound mapping systems, which are important in reading, writing and spelling.

Some of Stein's work, especially the suggested treatment with eye patching of a non-referent (dominant) eye, has proved controversial. He suggested that, at the critical age of 6–9 years, it is important that one eye learns to fixate, i.e. uniocular control, and that eye patching can be of a great help in developing binocular convergence and tracking.

It is also unfortunate that, as is often the case, the press and others take on complex theoretical notions, which are well documented and researched by people such as Stein, and use them to suggest an immediate 'quick fix' or treatments.

In the case of the cerebellar function, there were some attempts many years ago to prescribe travel sickness pills for people with dyslexia and, in the case of eye patching, I have had children in the past who have been at the school and have had eye patches. One boy in particular lost the eye-patch glasses in the first week and never wore them. When returning to the research centre, it was remarked how well he had done in improving reading and spelling and this was obviously the result of eye patching. In reality, it was the consequence of the hard work that he had done with the teachers. There had been no question about how long he had worn the eye-patch glasses! I have also had individuals who have been diagnosed as dyslexic on the basis of their binocular instability, rather than their reading, writing and spelling performance, which I think is putting the 'cart before the horse'.

Both the cerebellar and visual transient explanations are, however, persuasive because they try to explain many elements of dyslexia, not just reading or aspects of spelling. They are supported by evidence and it would be foolish to ignore them. I do not see that these theories, or others we have or will review, as necessarily mutually exclusive. If we view dyslexia as a syndrome, there may well be children who have more visually-oriented problems, or those with more difficulties in the motor area. I have commented above that I have known children with dyslexia who do not have poor balance, and also those whose binocular instabilities do not seem to feature as important in their own written language development. I could equally comment that I have known children with dyslexia who do well on phonological tests, which would cast doubt on the phonological weakness hypothesis. We are not talking about one sole cause, but a set of contributing factors that may be more important in a given case. We are more likely to discover a 'cause' in an individual – it is when we then generalize to all people with dyslexia that we have problems!

Further reading

Dyslexia, volumes 5.2 and 5.3 (published by Wiley), for papers on cerebellar and visual transient systems. For general reading on biological basis and neuropsychology of dyslexia:

Hulme C, Snowling M, eds (1997) *Biology, Cognition and Intervention*. London: Whurr Publishers, Chapters 1–4.

Pavlides G, Fisher D (1986) *Dyslexia, Neuropsychology and Treatment*. Chichester: Wiley, Chapters 4–6.

Pumfrey P, Reason R (1991) *Specific Learning Difficulties*. Windsor: NFER-Nelson, Chapters 9–11.

Robertson J (2000) *Dyslexia and Reading: A neuropsychological approach*. London: Whurr Publishers.

Stein J (1991) *Vision and Visual Dyslexia*. Basingstoke: Macmillan.

Thomson ME (1990) *Developmental Dyslexia*. London: Whurr, Chapter 3.

CHAPTER 7

Models of reading and spelling

As I have stated earlier, I look on dyslexia as an individual difference in learning style. One implication of this is that we should look at the learning task (written language) that we expect children to acquire so easily at the age of 5 or 6. If we take a kind of 'skills analysis' approach, we need to examine the written language system and look at the kinds of skills that are required of a young child (and indeed a mature reader), before we are able to look at what might go wrong in the acquisition of written language. It is important for teachers to understand the nature of the reading and spelling process, as well as how it develops in children. There is surprisingly little of this, in my experience, in teacher training. It seems fundamental to me that we look at the processes involved in what we are going to teach, not only to provide us with an understanding of what is required but also to examine the areas where some children might find certain skills particularly difficult.

Written language system

Written language is essentially a form of representation of ideas. Figure 7.1 illustrates some examples. There are both indirect and direct ways of accessing an idea that needs to be communicated. In a picture representation, we see what we observe directly and the idea is manifest, depending on the observer's world knowledge, semantic memory or cognitive process. In speech, there is also a direct representation by auditory input. This is non-durable, however, and as we listen to speech we forget what is said and, of course, it is open to interpretation later as a result of our relatively weak memory systems. The development of written language, where speech is represented as a durable and permanent record, has – some writers argue – given rise to modern civilization. However, this is a very indirect representation and the reader has to make a connection between how the speech, or the idea, is represented and how the reading

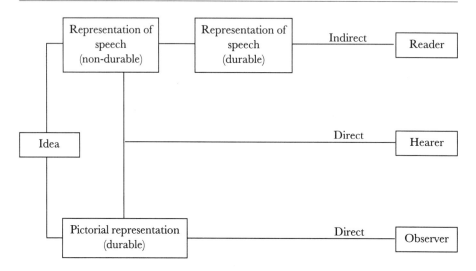

Figure 7.1 Representation of ideas.

system actually works. As you will see, this indirect representation of the ideas that we wish to communicate can lead to problems in some orthographies.

One problem, particularly in the case of western written language development, has been increasing arbitrariness. Most writers agree that spoken language is the prime symbol system. It appears to be biologically based, or certainly human beings are programmed to acquire spoken language at an early age. People still claim that one of the distinctions between animals and human beings is the fact that humans can use spoken language, and the interrelationship of speech, language and thought was one that gave rise to a great deal of speculation and research in linguistic writings both philosophically and psychologically. What is clear in the context here is that the alphabetical system has been invented by human beings and as such is a secondary symbol system. Many major civilizations in the world have developed their own written language systems, and as spoken language systems have changed so the representations of those spoken language systems by the written form have been different. Gradually, however, there has been a move from visual representations, i.e. drawing a picture of an idea, e.g. a picture of a cat when communicating the idea of the furry feline creature that we keep as a pet. The next stage appears to be the development of pictograms similar to some of the Chinese ideograms. Sometimes these are developed into syllabaries, where a particular ideogram or picture system represents a syllable in spoken language, and finally into alphabet where individual letters or combinations of letters represent sounds. In English, an example of western orthography, we have 26 symbols which represent over 40 phonemes. A phoneme is, of course, the distinctive sound in a particular spoken language that has a separate entity or meaning. However, for a young child, the individual letters are arbitrary in the first instance, i.e. they are meaningless. Furthermore, we combine letter combinations into different orders to give us different words. Figure 7.2 illustrates some of the difficulties this can cause children and is an example I have used before (Thomson, 1990).

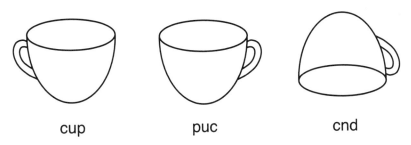

Figure 7.2 Picture and letters representing cup.

In Figure 7.2, we see that letter order and direction are very different from the idea of shape and size constancies. A perceptual constancy is what we learn in the first part of our life, i.e. that looking at objects in the environment from different angles does not cause them to become a different object or a different sound or a different element of another object or idea. Thus, looking at a cup from a different angle or from further away gives a different image on our retina, but it is still called a cup. However, with letters we start to change the labels with slightly different features. A 'b' and a 'd' have different sounds and different phonemic representations in written language. Thus, to represent an object such as a cup with letters, we have nonsensical pronunciations when looking at the word from a different angle or back to front. This is, of course, something that many children have difficulty with initially, but overcome. The dyslexic child may continue to have problems in this area.

The notion of the difference between a direct or visual route to meaning, as used by something like a Chinese pictogram, and an indirect route to reading via a phonemic or alphabetical system (credited to the Phoenicians) is the key difference seen by many theories in written language development.

Before we look at stage analysis and dual route theories of reading, it is worth examining some terminology. When reading a word we can look at it as a whole visual or global system and go straight to meaning, e.g. *string*, or we could divide it into intrasyllabic units such as *str + ing* or individual grapheme–phoneme relationships such as *s-t-r-i-n-g*, where we have to recognize individual letters given the sound and then blend them together. These phonological skills are a key process in learning to read and use alphabetical systems; we return to them in much more detail when we look at reading and spelling development and the phonological deficit model of dyslexia. Table 7.1 gives some ideas of particular examples of important units within written language.

Table 7.1 Examples of written language units

Word	Syllable	Onset and rime	Phoneme
dog	dog	d-og	d-o-g
string	string	str-ing	s-t-r-i-n-g
magnet	mag'net	m-ag'n-et	m-a-g-n-e-t

It is worth commenting, in passing, that children find it quite difficult to isolate individual phonemes in words before they are about 7, and onset and rime units and syllable units are much easier to divide. This is a key feature of teaching younger children.

One of the problems in describing theories on the reading and spelling process is that there are so many different levels and tasks to which we can refer to, e.g. take the English National Curriculum on this issue. The notion that you can divide written language skills into simply reading, writing, and speaking and listening is far too simplistic. As a practical example, we can have a dyslexic child who may be at a very high level in terms of attainment targets when it comes to understanding different genres, being aware of characterization, using description and awareness of poetry. However, his or her mechanical reading skills may be very weak and therefore these higher-order skills cannot be accessed, not because of an inability to do them but as a result of problems in letter–sound decoding. Table 7.2 illustrates this problem with reference to reading. Table 7.2 shows reading skills divided into, very broadly, two components: so-called mechanical, i.e. decoding or phonological skills, and lexical or higher-order skills – to do with the word. We can see under each of these the different levels of skill and expertise that might be required. To include all of these different areas in one unified theory of reading and spelling would be very difficult, and most of the reading and spelling theories tend to focus on the process of letter, word and sentence recognition. It is not the purpose here, and it would take up to two or three volumes, to review all of the different reading and spelling models that are current. What I

Table 7.2 Mechanical and higher-order skills in reading

Reading skills comments

Mechanical (decoding / phonological)

Recognition of 'text'	Includes left/right scanning, recognition of word/line units, top/bottom direction, pages, etc. This simple stage cannot be taken for granted in the dyslexic child
Basic sight vocabulary	High-frequency irregular words read. Able to recognize common vocabulary fluently without sounding out
Simple grapheme–phoneme skills	Common word units recognized, e.g. consonant blends, vowel–sound combinations
Phonic analysis skills	Identification of word units, 'sounding' out skills, blending and syllabification skills
Simple punctuation	Recognition of punctuation and its implication in reading aloud
Higher order (lexical)	
What are books, sentences, paragraphs and illustrations?	That books relate to communication, spoken language and can tell stories. Again this cannot be taken for granted
Use of context	Being able to follow the gist; expecting the next stage; what that part of the book is about
Use of inference	What the book suggests about other things; understand more sophisticated vocabulary, analogy and meaning
'Linguistic' fluency	Using punctuation appropriately; reading aloud with expression; 'skimming' for key meanings

hope to do is to present a skeleton of some examples of approaches that will give the reader an insight into the sorts of skills involved in written language acquisition.

Routes to reading

A useful approach to the processes involved in reading and spelling is that of stage analysis. Most stage models assume that there is some initial visual processing, followed by decoding visual input into a sound relating to speech and finally into semantic (meaning) and syntactic (grammar) components. The study of language – linguistics – has traditionally been divided into phonology (the sounds involved), syntax (grammar or structure of the language), semantics (the meaning and use of words) and aspects of metalinguistics (awareness of your own use of language and also non-verbal communication).

Figure 7.3 presents a simple example of how this is proposed. The lines separating the words, i.e. /Jane and Fred/ – /fell asleep/ –/in the

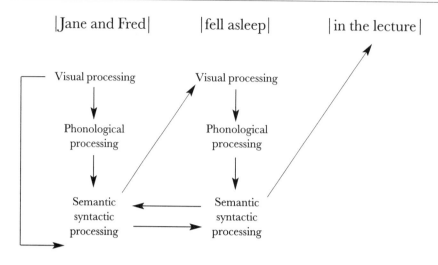

Figure 7.3 Stage analysis model in reading.

lecture/, represent saccades or eye movements, e.g. how much visual information can be taken in when reading the text. There is the implication that this has to be decoded, and the line from visual processing to semantic/syntactic processing implies a direct route to reading, whereas going through visual processing to phonological to the final stage implies some kind of indirect route. Semantic and/or syntactical processing can also help in predicting what the next input might be, hence the arrows down to the next chunk of visual processing.

This kind of approach has been formalized into the dual route to reading. It is interesting to note in passing that these models have, to some extent, been developed from observing people with acquired dyslexia, i.e. individuals who had a stroke or similar damage to parts of the brain that are responsible for written language learning. It has been observed that patients can produce different kinds of reading and spelling behaviour, e.g. some may be able to read irregular words well, whereas others have greater difficulty with non-words. Being able to read an irregular word implies going directly from input to meaning, whereas reading a non-word implies that we have to go through a grapheme to phoneme, i.e. a letter-to-sound correspondence route. The way that people produce differential responses has led to classification of acquired dyslexias into phonological and surface dyslexias, as a result of differing performance on non-words, regular words and irregular words. A typical example of a dual route theories to reading is illustrated in Figure 7.4, which presents a model for the understanding of decoding of both the spoken word and the printed word. In both cases, there is a spoken response going through

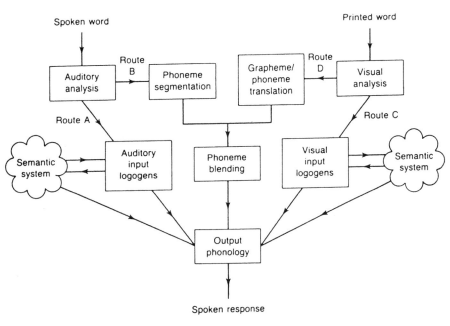

Figure 7.4 Examples of 'dual route' model of reading. Adapted from Snowling (1987) with permission.

to the box at the bottom called 'output phonology'. Output phonology is essentially the postulated cognitive or brain/thought process involved in putting together the sounds before making a speech utterance. In itself, this is a huge area of psychological interest and research!

In the flow charts going from both the spoken word and the printed word, there is a semantic system. Again, for the purposes of this model, this is just a nebulous and uncharted system that understands words and the context of words, and uses long-term memory and syntactical and semantic–linguistic systems to understand the input, whether through the spoken or the printed word, i.e. meaning. The two systems depart on the modality in which the words are presented. In the case of the spoken word, there is some preliminary auditory analysis and, in the case of the printed word, some visual analysis. If we focus on the printed word in this context, we can see that after visual analysis there are two systems labelled 'Route C' and 'Route D'. Route C is essentially the direct, or so-called Chinese, route to reading. In this, before visual analysis there is a direct link to the meaning system, involving a mechanism called a visual input logogen. Cognitive psychologists are very fond of developing terms that undertake various tasks, but no one knows the detail of what is going on. In this context, the logogen is simply a mechanism for recognition of visual input, i.e. it is something more than the recognition of what something looks like. For example, we might see the shape of a letter or a word in the abstract, but not recognize it as a letter or a word. The visual input logogen recognizes the letters, letter combinations and whole words. There is an access to the meaning system or the so-called internal lexicon. A lexicon is essentially a form of dictionary that is held somewhere in the cognitive system.

From this immediate recognition of the word, the sounds are assembled and the spoken response made. Thus, looking at a word such as *frog*, the letters are recognized as a whole word and there is access to the notion of a small, green, amphibious creature found in a pond, for example, and the word *frog* is said immediately. This is the way in which most adults, it is postulated, read. We tend to skim, read rapidly and go directly from the visual input to meaning without any indirect or decoding component.

Where we start using an indirect route is where we have difficult words. If we look at 'Route D', we see the visual analysis inputs into a box called 'grapheme–phoneme translation'. Essentially this is the alphabet system, and what we are doing is giving the letters their names or sounds. Sometimes this might be individual letters given individual sounds, such as *f-r-o-g*, or it might be various units, e.g. onset and rime like *fr-og* or blend plus vowel as in *fro-g*, and various combinations of these with longer multisyllabic words. This, therefore, goes through to a box called phoneme blending.

In this instance the letters that are recognized and held in short-term memory are blended together, e.g. *fr-og* or *f-r-o-g* to *frog*, etc. Finally, the word is spoken, and at this stage the semantic system kicks in, as it were. In other words, the word is now finally recognized as the small, green, amphibious creature found in a pond. This route, it is suggested, is the so-called Phoenician or indirect route and is used in the acquisition of reading. (Phoenicians are credited with inventing the alphabet.) When we come across a word that is not immediately recognized, we can use this grapheme–phoneme translation or the alphabet system route to work out what the word says. At that point, the pronunciation can be matched to our own internal lexicon or semantic system, to see whether the meaning can be understood. Obviously a non-word such as *spod* could be read through this system. Here, we do not find a semantic or dictionary entry, and therefore the word has no meaning. On the other hand, we might find a word we read that did not have a dictionary allocation, but was, in fact, a real word that we did not know. Thus, if the word *clan*, which is a relatively simple word to decode, was read by a young child, he or she may not have it in his or her internal lexicon and therefore would not be able to access its meaning. Nevertheless it is, of course, a real word. So, one notion is that a child acquires reading in the early stages, when the internal lexicon is not large, by the grapheme–phoneme translation route; similarly in spelling we would expect the reverse to occur, i.e. a sound to be assembled, put together with a letter combination or grapheme, and then to be spelt in a similar way.

As adults, we might sometimes use this indirect route, e.g. I read a lot of fantasy and, occasionally, if I come across a word such as 'Strakenoris' that I recognize as the Elf Queen, I might not bother to sound it out to myself. However, if I was reading it aloud I would have to pronounce it. Similarly, if reading a fantasy tale set in Celtic times, I might use Celtic pronunciations, if they were given in the book's appendix as 'how to pronounce Celtic orthography'. Here I would have to use an alphabetical or indirect route to work out what the pronunciations were. Mostly I might not bother to pronounce it correctly, but just go for the direct route to reading and understand what the word meant in context.

The fluency and the interactive component of an adult's written language system have given rise to the development of the stage models into slightly more sophisticated systems. The development of written language models has parallels with the development of cognitive psychology in other areas, such as memory, which we look at in Chapter 8. Basically, cognitive psychology has moved on from modal or box-like models to more interactive models, based on computer simulations and particularly connectionist theory. Without going into inappropriate detail here, connectionist theory looks at the way in which components of the cognitive system or brain interact. There has been a good deal of work on how neurons in the brain develop networks and interact with each other. In the context of written language, there have been developments of the notions of different kinds of processes involved in reading that interact with each other. A good example is given by Adams (1996) and illustrated in Figure 7.5.

The orthographic and phonological processes in Figure 7.5 are, I suppose, similar in many ways to the visual and auditory logogens mentioned earlier, and interact with the meaning processor. This involves both individual word meanings, i.e. the internal dictionary, and morphemic units, which would include such things as suffixes – -ed, -ing – or units of words that have particular meanings. Finally, these three main interactors, i.e. orthography, phonology and semantics or meaning, are dependent on the context, and here we have an attempt to extend models into more reality-based systems, including interpretation of the whole text, the context in which the words appear, etc. It also allows two way interaction.

Those readers who are teachers may notice interesting echoes in some of these models, e.g. the notion of a direct route to reading, i.e. looking at

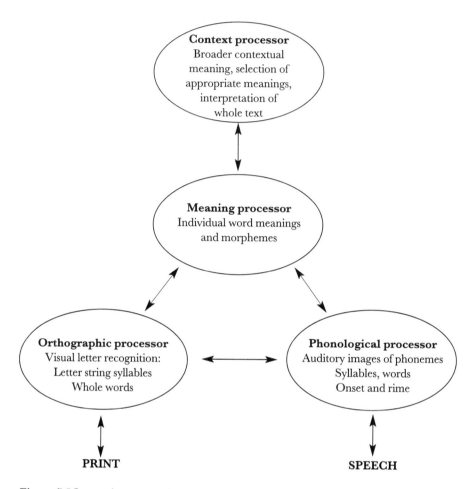

Figure 7.5 Interactive systems for written language. Source: Adams (1996).

the orthography (e.g. letters) and accessing the meaning of the word is essentially 'look and say'. Analysing the sounds, whether breaking them down into individual letters and their phonemes or letter combinations or building them up through blending to form the words, is essentially similar to 'phonics'. The notion of reading in context in terms of meaning is associated with so-called 'real reading'. All of these are particular fashions used in education from time to time, and one of the strengths of being aware of 'models' is that it makes us remember that all aspects are important. Of course, some children will have better skills in some areas and there are whole groups of children who have particular difficulty with aspects of comprehension. For the dyslexic child, the problem is mainly in the alphabetical decoding area. A number of researchers also argue that we cannot get on to the higher-order level recognition of words and their meanings without going through an alphabetical stage, or certainly the use of phonics and awareness of the relationship between the sound structure and the written language system.

It is worth making some additional comments on spelling. Spelling skills are not quite a simple difference between word recognition (reading) and production (spelling). They sometimes involve rather different skills. As in reading, spelling becomes lexical, i.e. word meaning with semantic and syntactic clues. There will, therefore, be a strong relationship between reading and spelling. On the other hand, we can also spell non-lexically, i.e. simply producing a sound, giving it a letter or letter combinations, and writing down non-words. In this, the focus is on sound–symbol relationships and the phonological and phonemic aspect of written language. Cognitive processing underlies both lexical and non-lexical skills, but there is also the so-called metacognitive, i.e. our knowledge about, and regulation of, spelling. To take a specific example in terms of suffix rules: before teaching dyslexic children, I was usually pretty good at spelling words such as 'hopped' or 'hoped', 'dinner' and 'diner', etc. This was an automatic or implicit skill that I had, but I did not have any orthographic knowledge about the rules involved. Once I began to teach dyslexic children, I soon learned that there was a rule (the doubling rule, which I won't go into here, but see Thomson and Watkins, 1999) to cover this situation. In other words, there was an explicit or metacognitive process that I could apply in working out how to spell words with suffixes and whether or not one doubled consonants. We can spend a good deal of time making the written language system very complex and Figure 7.6 presents some of the elements involved in the cognitive systems à propos spelling.

At the top of Figure 7.6 we have auditory input. This input can come from outside, if someone is asking us to spell a word and we have to write it down as in a spelling test, or internally if we are trying to create our own spellings. This implies some kind of phonological memory or loop system (see Chapter 8), which enables us to create these sounds internally. The processing system obviously involves short-term (or working) memory and attention to stimuli, as shown in the figure. The auditory input is then broadly divided into lexical and non-lexical systems, i.e. words and non-words if you like. I do not propose to go through the figure in great detail, but it is worth having a look through at all the various interactive (note that the arrows are two-way) aspects. Try to relate the various components to models that we have already discussed and those later in the chapter. You then might like to add your own ideas to make it even more complicated!

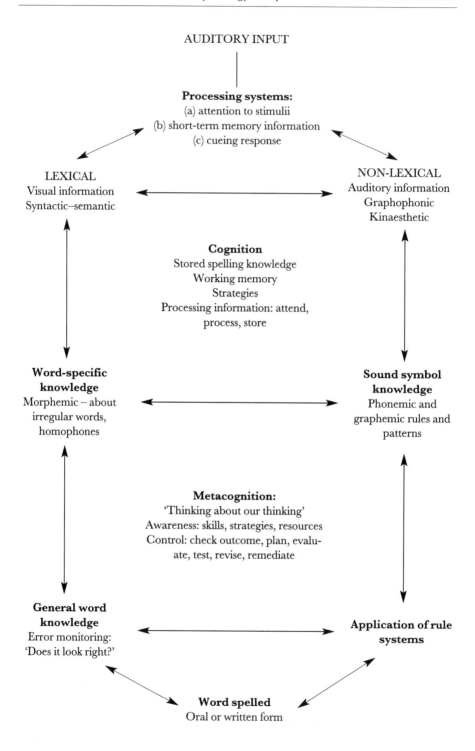

Figure 7.6 Example of cognitive processes involved in spelling.

This is not supposed to be a complete review, but I hope that it gives the reader some idea of the sorts of approaches involved in developing models of reading and spelling, and also some of the complexities.

The development of written language

We now turn to some approaches to the development of written language skills. As is often the case in developmental psychology, people try to look at stage developments in children. This essentially follows on from dear old Piaget and tries to place children in the context of their developing learning skills. The implication is that children move from simple to more complex skills, and it is quite interesting to note the parallels between proposed developmental stages in children and the various different stages involved in the models of reading and spelling processes. I am going to start off, unusually, with a summary at the beginning of this section on reading and spelling development so that the reader has a context.

Most developmental stage models of reading and spelling learning have early visual recognition of familiar assembled phonology (sound from speech represented as letters/words) as part of initial learning. This initially implies visual skills in which letter combinations that are learnt are recognized straightaway, but this obviously is a skill that needs to be acquired. The next stage is a letter-to-sound conversion process of some sort, leading to phonological processing. The phonological processing is related to phonemic awareness and has interactive links with short-term memory. Next there is development of the mental lexicon, i.e. a store of sight recognition words. The implication behind this is that there are dual routes with learning sight words via (1) grapheme–phoneme conversion or assembled phonology, i.e. letter combinations being put together, or (2) direct visual recognition and, finally, the relationship between semantic memory (understanding the word) and output phonology (saying the word). There is an assumption that new and unfamiliar words will be recognized by the grapheme–phoneme correspondence route. This will sound familiar, of course, and is essentially what is involved in some of the dual process and aspects of interactive reading processes that we have already looked at. However, let us turn back a bit and look at the development of these systems in written language learning.

One of the most influential and widely quoted stage models has been that of Frith (1985), developed from Marsh et al. (1981), who in turn was trying to develop a Piagetian approach to written language learning. It is surprising, in fact, how little research and theoretical modelling has been done on the written language learning process, as opposed to reading and spelling processes in adults. Table 7.3 shows the main elements of Frith's proposed stages.

Table 7.3 Three phases of reading development (Frith, 1985)

Stage 1 Logographic

Associate speech signs with symbols. Read as logograms. Shape recognition. Memory of environment. Particular words/spoken/written

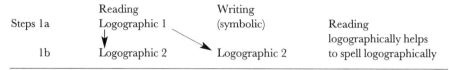

	Reading	Writing	
Steps 1a	Logographic 1	(symbolic)	Reading logographically helps
1b	Logographic 2	Logographic 2	to spell logographically

Stage 2 Alphabetical

Chunking letter sounds and morpheme identification. Grapheme–phoneme translation route, sound-to-letter correspondence; requires phonemic awareness, decoding novel words

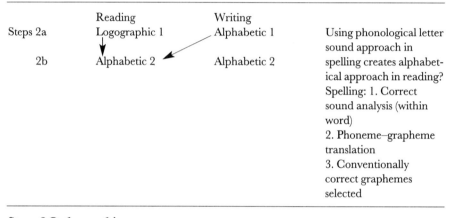

	Reading	Writing	
Steps 2a	Logographic 1	Alphabetic 1	Using phonological letter sound approach in
2b	Alphabetic 2	Alphabetic 2	spelling creates alphabetical approach in reading? Spelling: 1. Correct sound analysis (within word) 2. Phoneme–grapheme translation 3. Conventionally correct graphemes selected

Stage 3 Orthographic

Automatic recognition of graphemic clusters: -tion, etc. Access to lexical representations set up relating to letter-by-letter sequences, use of lexical analogies

	Reading	Writing	
Steps 3a	Orthographic 1	Alphabetical 3	Uses orthographic code first in reading then
3b	Orthographic 2	Orthographic 2	transfers/develops spelling

Broadly, there are three stages: logographic, alphabetical and orthographic. The logographic stage is at the very beginning of learning to recognize text and written material, in which children may recognize whole units, but very much in the context of the environment, e.g. a McDonald's sign may be recognized, as might Coca Cola. There would be no generalization from McDonald's to a word beginning with 'M', or from Coca Cola to words such as 'cocoa'. Children often reading particular words in the environmental context in which they occur. One of the interesting things about Frith's theory is that there is often interaction between one stage and another, e.g. reading words logographically can lead on to beginning to spell words, i.e. children copying down shapes and symbols that they see in the environment around them. The shapes can then be given names by parents, e.g. M for the M in McDonald's, and the letter is spelt. Reading therefore starts off the development of spelling skills. At the logographic stage, particular words can be recognized, remembered, read or spelt, but it is not until the alphabetical stage that the child starts to recognize new words, generalize and begin to develop implicit knowledge of letter–sound combinations.

In the alphabetical stage, children will start to break down letter sounds into longer units, identify units within words and, crucially, develop grapheme–phoneme translation route skills. In other words, they will be able to recognize individual letters in combination given the appropriate sounds. Underlying this, of course, is the implication that phonemic awareness and phonological skills are required. Table 3.2, p. 45, shows the sorts of phonological skills involved, as does Table 7.2, p. 95. Here, developing alphabetical skills begin to feed, from writing or spelling, into the alphabet. As we hear sounds, e.g. 'frog', and allocate particular letter combinations to them, that skill can be used in recognizing and decoding novel words in reading, e.g. the alphabetic 2 stage in reading.

In spelling, I have added three small stages: correct sound analysis within words, phoneme–grapheme translation, i.e. sound to letters, and finally selecting the conventionally correct graphemes. This is not easy for many children, and at the early stages of spelling can give rise to mistakes such as 'tese', 'cez', 'jes' or 'tz' for 'cheese', all of which are not random representations but approximations to the sound, and also more sophisticated attempts such as 'clend' for 'cleaned', 'jumt' for 'jumped', etc. Some phonological skills are clearly being used here. Choosing the correct orthography to represent a given sound becomes quite a problem for children with dyslexia, e.g. different 13-year-old children with dyslexia in my current teaching group gave the following spellings for 'shield': 'sheild', 'shild', 'shiel', 'sheld', 'sheeld', 'sheeyled', 'cheeld' and 'shiyeld'. Some of these indicate phonological problems, but most are reasonable representations of the word.

The next stage is the so-called orthographic stage. Here, recognition of graphemic clusters becomes much more automatic. There is an implicit, or sometimes explicit, awareness of what sound structures or letter combinations are common in a given language. There is access to lexical representations, i.e. word dictionaries, by relating to letter sequences, but also comparing words analogously. This sort of approach has been developed by other theorists such as Goswami (1986, 1988) (see page 107). In this case we have the development of reading skills, i.e.

beginning to recognize and internalize common spelling patterns. Vowel combinations, for example, are fiendish in English /a/ (play, maid, made, eight, great, etc.) and beginning to recognize the most common spellings of the letter sound in reading begins to develop into writing skills.

Frith has given us quite a neat way of examining developmental skills across time and also the interrelationship of spelling and reading. Of course, as Frith would be the first to acknowledge, it is not as simple as a stark three-stage system, but it does give us a clear relationship between the reading and spelling models that we have outlined previously and how they might develop in children. The notion of three stages has been taken on by a number of researchers and other aspects of written language learning have been looked at in more detail, e.g. Ehri (1991) examined the development of just sight vocabulary and knowledge of spelling. The stages are presented in Table 7.4.

Table 7.4 Three stages of sight reading

Sight reading (Ehri)	Parallel stages in spelling (Henderson)
*Emergent readers: no sound/symbol, visual aspects of word only	Pre-phonetic
*Phonetic cue reading: one or two specific cues, individual letters/blends give phonic clues	Semi-phonetic
Cipher sight word reading: stored in memory, spelling/phonological associations	Phonetic

*Instruction necessary, i.e. letters/phonemic segmentation.

Ehri proposes three stages in just the sight-reading aspect, although there are parallels between her approach and those of Frith and Henderson. According to Ehri, emergent readers select salient visual cues and associate these with words in memory. The cues bear no relationship to the sound. In the phonetic cue stage, letters that link spelling to word pronunciation are the associations used. Finally, readers learn more conventional ways of symbolizing sounds with letters, enabling readers to retrieve specific pronunciation and meaning as a whole. Cue readers would have problems with similarly spelt words. The spelling mentioned above refers to another stage analysis model, that of Henderson (1981). Henderson argues that the logographic stage would have to be very brief because there is soon development of phonological skills in spelling. She proposes a five-stage model, shown in Table 7.5, with illustrations of the kinds of mistakes that might be made.

Others, such as Goswami (e.g. 1988), have argued that children do not develop through discrete stages. She introduces the notion of lexical

Table 7.5 Henderson's Five-stage Model (Henderson, 1981)

1. Precommunicative
   Letters at random. Not representing sounds or words
2. Semi-phonetic
   Some awareness. 'R' for 'are'
3. Phonetic
   Representation of sounds, but what sequences are OK in English? 'ckut' for 'cut'
4. Transitional
   Conventional spelling and meaning. 'Eightee' for 'eighty' (earlier 'ate')
5. Correct
   Fewer errors, knowledge of orthography

analogy, and in particular the development of intrasyllabic skills in children. Goswami emphasizes the division between onset and rime, e.g. words such as *trap* can be divided into *t-r-a-p* or *tr-ap* or *tra-p* or *t-rap*. Note that 'rime' is vowel plus consonant. e.g. -ap in tr'ap. 'Rhyme' is two words that rhyme, not necessarily with the same orthography, e.g. pot/lot/yacht. She points to the research correlating rhyme detection with reading development, the former being a predictor of reading, and argues that onset and rime awareness appear before reading, e.g. during sound and word play. She also emphasizes the interrelationship, as we have seen earlier, between chronological development as a consequence of reading and spelling and vice versa, and argues that beginner readers start to use analogies between words, i.e. drawing parallels between, for example, *mean* and *heap, bead, beat, peak*, etc.

Again, those who are teachers will begin to recognize the notion of word families among this lexical analogy theory. Without being too cynical, in my experience cognitive and developmental, psychologists often reinvent the wheel, or more likely dress up relatively simple classroom concepts in complex cognitive psychology vocabulary!

As in the previous chapters, it is not my purpose to review all the theories of reading and spelling development, but it is worth finishing this section with a slightly more detailed reiteration of the commonalities of stage development theories (Table 7.6).

Table 7.6 Stage development: commonalities

Visual recognition	Familiar words/shapes: visualization, recognition
Alphabetic component	Phoneme→grapheme rules (phonological coding/short-term memory, phonemic awareness). 'Recognition→recall'
Storage of sight words	Mental lexicon, word understanding, orthography (conventional, morphemes, irregular patterns)

It may be seen that the three major components – visual recognition, alphabetical and sight word storage – have their echoes in the models of reading and spelling process outlined earlier. Basically, the notion is that children begin to learn to read and spell by recognizing familiar words and shapes, particularly using recognition and so-called visualization skills, i.e. what a word looks like and the shapes and visual elements of units. Then comes an alphabetical component involving phoneme-to-grapheme or grapheme-to-phoneme skills (depending on whether one is spelling or reading). The important implication here is that the phonological coding, short-term memory and phonemic awareness skills are all linked, and that there is a difference between recognition (reading) and recall (spelling). The alphabetical component, or phonics, as opposed to the 'look and say' or visual sight vocabulary component, would tend to come later, although of course, there is a good deal of overlap and these stages are not finite or particularly linked to any age group. In my experience some children with dyslexia may not reach the alphabetical stage until they are 13 or 14 (if at all!), a stage that some 5 and 6-year-olds will have reached.

Following these decoding skills, we have storage of sight words and the more contextually meaning oriented aspects of written language, which come at a later stage. These include the development of a mental lexicon or internal dictionary, understanding words and also the development of orthographic skills. This includes remembering irregular word patterns and also understanding conventional orthography such as -tion.

Those teachers experienced in helping dyslexic children or children with specific learning difficulties, using structured phonic programmes, will notice the very broad parallel between how these programmes develop and how reading and spelling are proposed to develop in children. Initially there is usually some attempt to teach a basic corpus of sight vocabulary. Then the phonic component starts off with simple phoneme–grapheme correspondence rules such as alphabet and consonant blends, and develops into more complicated rules involving phonemic awareness such as vowel combinations. This is followed by syllabification and segmentation skills in teaching multisyllable regular words, finally building up to spelling rules and use of more complex, irregular words as in the later stages of the stage development models.

We return to phonological skills in more detail when we examine theories of causes of dyslexia, focusing particularly on the core phonological deficit notion (see Chapter 9). However, as a taster for this discussion and to finish off the chapter, Table 7.7 illustrates the relationship between the development in phonological knowledge and how that relates to difficulties in some children with dyslexia.

Table 7.7 Phonological knowledge

Development	Some dyslexic children
Names of objects/events	Difficulties in naming, syllable omission, juxtaposition, substitution
Sound patterns → sounds in words	Vowel confusions within words, following speech difficulties
Segmentation → onset/rime → blend string into words	Sound-blending difficulties
Phonological recoding → link sounds/letters	Grapheme–phoneme correspondence
Orthographic knowledge (phonemic awareness) – automaticity – self-teaching, analogies – similarities	Short-term memory problems Lack of phonemic awareness

Further reading

More detailed descriptions of models and written language process can be found in:

Adams MJ (1996) *Beginning to Read: Thinking and learning about print*. Boston, MA: MET Press.
Perfetti C (1985) *Reading Ability*. New York: Oxford University Press.

For detail and/or sources for the development of written language and relevance to dyslexia can be found in:

Goswami U, Bryant PJ (1990) *Phonological Skills and Learning to Read*. Hillsdale, NJ: Lawrence Erlbaum.
Hulme C, Snowling MJ, eds (1997) *Dyslexia: Biology, cognition and intervention*. London: Whurr Publishers, Chapters 8, 4 and 11.
Snowling MJ (1987, 2001) *Dyslexia: A cognitive perspective*. Oxford: Blackwell.
Snowling MJ, Thomson ME (1992) *Dyslexia: Integrating theory and practice*. London: Whurr Publishers, Chapters 5–8.

CHAPTER 8

Models of memory

As well as obvious problems with reading and spelling, one of the key features of the dyslexic learner is problems with aspects of memory. In particular, these centre around short-term memory, in its relationship both to classroom instructions and organization and in particular to aspects of written language learning. Obviously, a failure to internalize or remember grapheme–phoneme rules or sound–symbol correspondence is a key feature of learning to read and part of the memory system. However, in addition we need to look at the naming problems that people with dyslexia manifest and their use of phonetic or phonological codes in short-term memory systems, and an overview of aspects of current thinking about human memory is essential if we are to understand the totality of the dyslexia syndrome. It is also on the syllabus of all the courses that deal with dyslexia, from certificate through diploma and postgraduate masters degrees! Inevitably, as in other cases of reviewing the psychology underlying dyslexia, we need to be selective. There is a mountain of psychological research, many books on memory (see further reading). The focus will be primarily on working memory (a way of conceptualizing short-term memory), but I make brief reference to other aspects of memory systems. We shall briefly review some of the more recent ideas in describing memory, but most have their roots in the idea of a modal memory system. This describes memory in terms of a series of stages, and a typical example is given in Figure 8.1.

Memory systems are very broadly divided into three areas sometimes referred to as the sensory register, short-term or working memory, and long-term memory. The sensory register is essentially a very brief store of uncoded visual and auditory information. There are, of course, sensory registers for other modalities, including kinaesthetic and all of our five senses, but there has been much less research and focus on these in the psychological literature. Basically, a sensory register decays rapidly but has quite a large capacity. A typical experiment demonstrating a visual

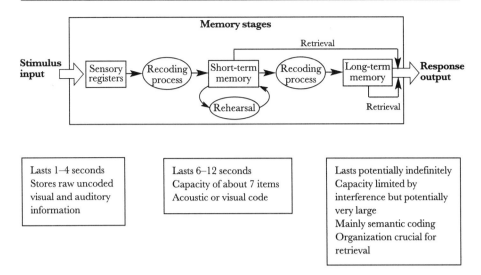

Figure 8.1 Multistore or modal model of memory.

sensory register (sometimes known as iconic memory) is a tachistoscopic task (Table 8.1): an array is presented very briefly (50 milliseconds) in a tachistoscope (a box-like machine where stimuli are presented for someone to look at through a viewer). Subjects are asked to report what they remember once the light has been turned off. On average they remember about four to five items before their memory of the numbers decays. However, if the subjects are asked to read off the top, bottom or middle line, i.e. their memory is cued by a high, medium or low tone, they are usually able to remember three to four of any line cued (despite not knowing which line was going to be cued). The implication for this is that the whole array is available very briefly in our sensory register or iconic memory, but because it decays so rapidly we are only able to remember a few of the numbers unless we are cued specifically to focus on one or two areas. If we do this, we are able to read these off quite happily, while the others decay.

When we look at the relationship between memory and dyslexia, we see that there is some evidence for problems in certain aspects of the sensory register, particularly naming, but in general terms this is not now

Table 8.1 Array of 12 digits presented by a tachistoscope

3	1	8	4
2	6	5	2
9	4	7	9

a primary area of research into dyslexia and its relationship to reading difficulties.

The modal model shows a short-term memory system that involves re-coding material, both for input and output in short-term memory, and there is a need for rehearsal. The capacity in short-term memory systems is very limited. Acoustic or visual (and other) codes are used, and as Figure 8.1 illustrates, this lasts about 6–12 seconds. Finally, there is a long-term memory system that potentially has a very large capacity. One of the main problems concerns retrieval of information from the long-term memory stores.

Traditionally, short-term memory has seemed to be mainly an acoustic or visual storage system, whereas the long-term memory system is mainly semantic. Also, originally there were proposals that the short-term memory system was essentially an electrical feedback system, i.e. material was kept in short-term memory by electrical activity or traces in the central nervous system, in particular the brain, whereas long-term memory was seen to be a more permanent store. This was postulated to be the result of biochemical changes in the ribonucleic acid (RNA) in the cells of the brain's neurons. It is beyond the scope of this book to pursue these ideas further; instead I should like to present a more up-to-date picture of memory systems, and then we can focus in particular on working memory.

Figure 8.2 is an expanded, slightly different version of the modal memory system. We see in this that there is still a sensory memory, which

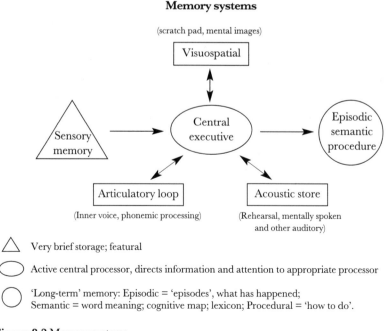

Memory systems

(scratch pad, mental images)

Visuospatial

Sensory memory

Central executive

Episodic semantic procedure

Articulatory loop

Acoustic store

(Inner voice, phonemic processing)

(Rehearsal, mentally spoken and other auditory)

△ Very brief storage; featural

◯ Active central processor, directs information and attention to appropriate processor

◯ 'Long-term' memory: Episodic = 'episodes', what has happened; Semantic = word meaning; cognitive map; lexicon; Procedural = 'how to do'.

Figure 8.2 Memory systems.

involves very brief storage and looks at the features of input coming to us from the environment. We then have the working memory system that consists of a central executive. This is an active central processor, to make a computer analogy, and directs information to other processors and also into the memory system. You can see that there are interactive loops between the central executive and the articulatory loop, the visuospatial processor and the acoustic store. These involve, respectively, the so-called inner voice or phonemic processing, a visuospatial 'scratch pad' dealing with mental images and an acoustic store dealing with rehearsal, and mentally spoken and other auditory materials. We return to these areas in more detail later (see page 114).

Finally, there is long-term memory. This is broadly agreed to be divided into at least three components. One is the episodic which, as the name implies, is essentially what has happened in the past and the 'episodes' in one's life, e.g. what happened when you went to the fair in Bognor! Semantic memory deals with word meaning. It is related to what is sometimes known as the cognitive map, i.e. our awareness of the world around us, its structure, assumed and common memories, and knowledge. In addition, semantic memory deals with the lexicon, i.e. our internal dictionary. There are obviously important components of accessing the lexicon in both reading and spelling, as well as our language work, and this is an area that has some impact on dyslexic diffi- culties. Thirdly, there is procedural memory, i.e. how to do things or procedures. This might be things such as boiling an egg, changing the carburettor on the car, etc. It is interesting to note that procedural memory can consist of a string of small items or just one overall proce- dure, depending on how one codes and memorizes, e.g. the procedure to 'boil an egg' is essentially just one unit of memory for myself and most readers. On the other hand, for a young person away from home for the first time, 'boil an egg' is not one procedure – it is a whole series of differ- ent ones: find a saucepan, put water in it, put it on to boil, place egg in saucepan, time egg, etc., etc.!

We now look in more detail at working memory, which is the system that is most relevant to dyslexia. Working memory is essentially what we might call the 'desktop' of the brain. It keeps track of what we do moment by moment and organizes and directs our attention. It has a number of features. The first is its relatively limited capacity, i.e. it deals with imme- diate past experience. Although all senses input information into the working memory system, there is also a selection and attentional compon- ent here, as a result of the limited capacity. In addition, it is a temporary system. The purpose of this seems to be to avoid 'crowding'. Obviously if we were unable to forget information coming in to us at any particular moment, we would have difficulty dealing with everyday events. An example that illustrates dyslexic difficulties came from a boy I taught recently. Although very severely dyslexic, he was able, given time, to undertake multisyllable words. However, with a simpler example such as *magnet*, if I gave him another word before he had finished processing the first, it was almost as though he was unable to use selective attention or avoid the second word crowding out the first. Thus, he would get very frustrated and annoyed with me if I gave another word before he had finished processing the first one, and sometimes the second one would interfere with the first, so that he might write *mag-fem* if the second word given was *poem*.

To return to the working memory, it is also an active system, i.e. material must be combined, manipulated and interpreted by the central executive. Figure 8.3 illustrates a slightly different way of conceptualizing working memory. It may be seen, for the purposes of illustration here, that the input is just auditory and visual. The phonological loop is connected with speech and sounds, and the visual cache with writing

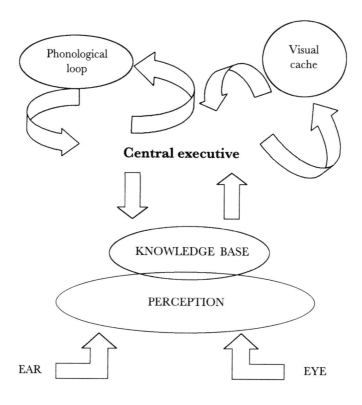

Figure 8.3 Representation of working memory.

output. The central executive also has the function of allocating inputs and directing operations. There is a connection between what is referred to as a knowledge base. This can also refer to information from long-term memory and semantic and lexical systems, as well as procedures and episodes. Figure 8.4 breaks these elements down into further detail, with some additional notes.

The central executive is seen to be modality free, whereas the phonological loop and the visuospatial scratch pad are linked to auditory and visual information, respectively. Again, we use various terminologies here – visual cache, visuospatial scratch pad, etc. The visual cache appears to have a number of different functions. One is concerned with visual appearance and location. If you imagine shutting your eyes and then picking up an object in front of you, this is essentially an aspect of visual imagery. You are remembering where the object is and can put your hands on it without looking. Similarly, the sort of memory required to describe a scene that you have looked at is involved in this aspect of working memory. Information is held and new information is also generated from a knowledge base, i.e. having seen a double-decker bus when looking at a scene, but also your knowledge of double-decker buses, the fact that they tend to be red, etc., all help in the description of the scene.

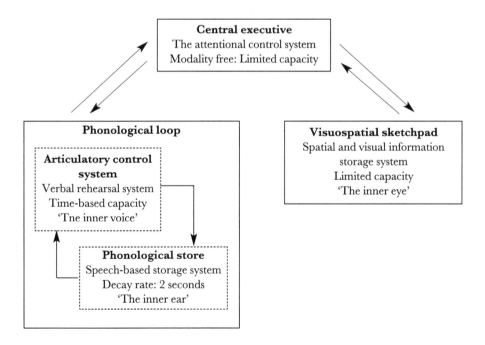

Figure 8.4 Working memory model.

Visual cache is also involved in so-called mental discovery. You might want to imagine some shapes or, if you are given some shapes, you can recombine them in different ways to produce something else. This form of mental imagery may also transfer to the phonological loop if you are naming something. You might want to try using a large rectangle, a triangle and three smaller rectangles of the same size. If you recombine these using the triangle as a roof, the large rectangle as walls and the three smaller rectangles as a door and two windows, we now have a new object that we can label 'house'. The phonological loop is of particular interest to us because it has relationships with language, reading and dyslexia, in particular. It is generally divided into articulatory control and a phonological store. The articulatory control system is described as the so-called 'inner voice'. This is essentially a verbal rehearsal system, which is linked to some vocal activities. Importantly, it is a serial and temporal system, i.e. it maintains things in order and concerns time-based decay. These are key features of some difficulties that dyslexics have.

The phonological store, on the other hand, is a speech-based storage system. The so-called 'inner ear' is less involved with articulatory rehearsal. It decays quite rapidly, but as indicated in Figure 8.4 it can be recycled through the articulatory control system. The phonological loop is quite clearly linked to our speech system, and indeed to language. There is also an additional assumed coding system within the phonological loop. Phonological coding can involve two elements. One is the loudness and acoustic pitch of auditory stimuli coming in and the second, importantly as far as written language is concerned, is phonemic speech sounds, i.e. what are the important, significant sounds in a given language and, in the case of reading, how do these relate to the graphemes used to represent them. Phonological coding is quite clearly related to aspects of phonemic awareness and phonological skills that we have described in assessment procedures and in the nature of written language systems (see page 91).

There are some quite interesting relationships between so-called span tasks and language in the phonological loop, e.g. there is a good correlation between speech rate and digit span. Many dyslexics have problems with digit span, and it is also interesting to note that a good deal of research has shown that remembering a sequence of longer words is more difficult than remembering a sequence of shorter words in general. This appears to be linked with the memory capacities involved in the articulatory control system. The longer the words, the more the system is being stretched in its capacity. We can see the resonance with dyslexia – if there are short-term memory weaknesses, it is not surprising that long words can present difficulties and that dyslexics can have segmentation problems.

There are also some quite interesting effects that can occur in labora-
tory-based tasks, one of which is so-called 'articulatory suppression'. Try
counting a simple number sequence in your head – say 1 to 10 or 10 to
20. This is an easy task but, if at the same time you repeat the word 'the' –
'the' – 'the' out loud, you will find that the task becomes much more difficult! This illustrates quite nicely the limited capacity of some of these
systems, and perhaps may give an insight into what could be happening
with dyslexic children. Perhaps asking a person with dyslexia to spell is
equivalent to giving him or her an articulatory suppression task. Obviously, articulatory control, the phonological code and the phonological
store are all aspects required in written language learning. Segmentation
and pronunciation tasks are linked to articulatory control; giving a
grapheme a sound code is phonological coding and remembering that
link is the phonological store.

One suggestion is that the phonological loop is a key element of learning to read, but perhaps when reading becomes difficult it is also a system
back-up. There is evidence to suggest that when reading becomes difficult there are subvocalized larynx movements in individuals, and articulatory suppression tasks decrease comprehension. In general, an
articulatory suppression task enables us to remember the gist of what we
have read if we are fluent readers, but the exact wording suffers.

There have also been attempts to link the categorizations from experimental psychology of working memory to research in neuropsychology,
e.g. in brain imaging techniques using the cerebral blood flow, we can
find evidence for different neuropsychological systems. These imaging
techniques rely on an increase in blood flow to areas of the brain that are
excited or fired up when particular tasks are being performed. We examined some examples of research in Chapter 6, but in this case using PET
(positron emission tomography), i.e. looking at blood flow and getting
colour-coded brain maps, we find evidence for a phonological loop being
divided into a memory store and a rehearsal system (phonological store
and articulatory rehearsal, respectively). In addition, mental rehearsal of
letters seems to fire up Broca's area which is involved in speech production, whereas letter memory is related to the supramarginal gyrus (see
Chapters 5 and 6, pages 56 and 67).

There are, of course, other models of human memory systems. There is
no space to summarize these, but it may be worth just mentioning a couple
so that interested readers can follow this up from Further reading later.
Two slightly different approaches to memory are the adaptive control of
thought (ACT) system and the parallel distributive processing (PDP)
system linked to neural networks. The ACT system can be summarized in
terms of its general framework (Figure 8.5). The main elements are

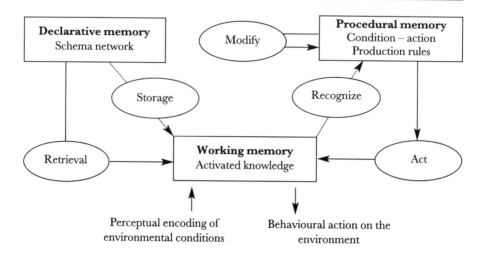

Figure 8.5 A general framework for the ACT system, identifying the major structural components and their interlinking processes.

particularly associated with long-term memory and look at a number of processes, including encoding, storage, retrieval, recognition, action, performance and modification, which are seen as interlinking processes.

The PDP approach looks at the development of neural networking ideas in neuropsychology, as well as in cognitive psychology. Basically, the idea is that, as neurons seem to have multi-connections with each other and build up networks, perhaps our memory system works in similar kinds of ways. PDP research gets quite complicated and builds up mathematical models of the extent and way in which neurons are weighted. The idea is that our experience and things that we learn will result in the neural nets in our brain learning. The way this is done is by the activation traces between neurons being easier to excite because of previous experience and excitations. This results in certain input patterns that are weighted, so information from minimal cues can give rise to memories, etc. The advantage of this kind of approach is that it explains how much of our brain is redundant – the notion of 'redundant encoding' is an important component of the PDP approach. It also takes into account so-called graceful degradation, i.e. that our memory systems do not suddenly stop but we can gradually forget things over time.

As far as the relationship between PDP and written language is concerned, there are some quite interesting research approaches coming out. Indeed the following discussion could equally be in Chapter 7. The most influential model is that of Seidenberg and McClelland (1989), although a review by Snowling (1998b) is the most relevant to dyslexia. In their connectionist or PDP model, multi-level processing assigns weights to the representation of words. Two representational units are proposed – orthographic and phonological units. An orthographic unit is the coding of letters in printed words and the phonological unit is the coding of word pronunciation. The former is seen to be an input unit and the latter output, both connected via intermediate or hidden units.

Research looking at the recognition of triple letter strings in a given word, e.g. -ma, mak, ake, ke-, has examined the sequence of features that activates the unit. It has been found that the brain responds to many different input triples, i.e. recognition of orthographic units. These can then access phonological, i.e. pronunciation or output, units each of which will specify a triplet of phonetic features. Researchers have constructed computer networks, based on the above principles, that behave in similar ways to human subjects undertaking the same task. In particular, computer models, after training, i.e. recognizing specific triplets, can generalise to words that have not been explicitly taught. The above model looks purely at word recognition and it is recognized that semantic information is also used during reading; later models have incorporated this.

Snowling (1998b) states that such models can be a useful metaphor for the reading process because they are sensitive to the irregularities of the English language and, as they are explicit, can be easily tested. Thus the observation that children use rime as opposed to phonemes (i.e. fr-og rather than f-r-o-g) more easily in English is predicted by the connectionist model because more 'transparent' languages, i.e. those with more regular sound–symbol correspondence, are more easily learnt at the phoneme level.

As far as dyslexia is concerned, we have the possibility of problems in either or both orthographic or phonological units. Computer modelling of coarse coding of output units can be shown to learn less effectively or generalize less well. So, we have specific deficits at verbal short-term memory that link to the phonological theories of dyslexia, but also leave open some of the perceptual or visual processing difficulties that might operate in some people with dyslexia.

We have not touched on many other aspects of memory, including schemas, semantic memory, everyday memory, including eye witness accounts, meta-memory, etc. These are really beyond the scope of this book, and the interested reader is referred to Further reading. The purpose of this chapter has been to provide an outline of those concepts that are needed to understand memory and phonological difficulties in dyslexia.

Further reading

Baddeley A (1990) *Human Memory: Theory and practice*. Basingstoke: Lawrence Erlbaum.

Baddeley A (1999) *Essentials of Human Memory*. Hove: Psychology Press.

Cohen G, Kiss G, Le-Voi M. (1993) *Memory: Current issues*. Buckingham: Open University Press.

CHAPTER 9

Phonological and memory deficits in dyslexia

A core phonological deficit

In this chapter we turn to the cognitive level of dyslexia, examining in particular the notion of a phonological deficit and its overlap with verbal short-term memory difficulties in children with dyslexia. Figure 9.1 shows a typical causal model of dyslexia resulting from phonological deficit, as put forward by Frith (1999).

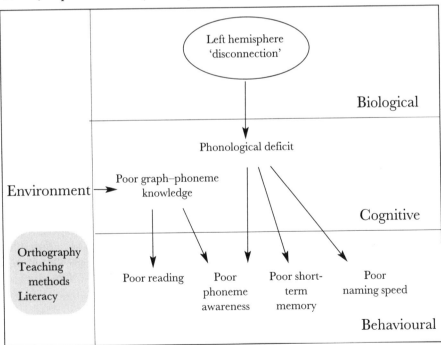

Figure 9.1 A casual model of dyslexia as a result of a phonological deficit. From Frith (1999) Paradoxes in Developmental Dyslexia, John Wiley and Sons. Reproduced with permission.

In Figure 9.1 unspecified assumptions about the biological basis are made, e.g. left hemisphere disconnection or difference in processing (see Chapter 6). This gives rise to a phonological deficit, which can result in poor grapheme–phoneme knowledge, i.e. difficulties in learning the alphabet. Of course there will be an environmental part to play here because, if you do not get taught letter–sound correspondence, you are not going to have that knowledge. This component is acknowledged in Figure 9.1. Also included are the type of orthography, e.g. the difficulty of English against, say, more regular spelling in Spanish or a pictograph system in Chinese. This phonological deficit gives rise to some of the things that you observe in children with dyslexia. In Figure 9.1 particular examples are given of poor reading, phonemic awareness and poor naming speed. Poor short-term memory is also mentioned as a result of a phonological deficit. The directionality of this particular relationship is something that we discuss in more detail later in the chapter. Also of note are literacy values, i.e. expectations of learning from home or at school, which are all important elements associated with school learning and its relationship to written language learning.

Before we look at an overview of the evidence for a phonological deficit in children with dyslexia, it is worth examining one or two methodological issues. At this point, it is also worth reminding readers that they should be familiar with the earlier chapters on the development of written language learning in children, as well as models of reading, writing and spelling process. A good deal of research has pinpointed the relationship between early rhyming skills and future reading, and Figure 9.2 illustrates elements of this.

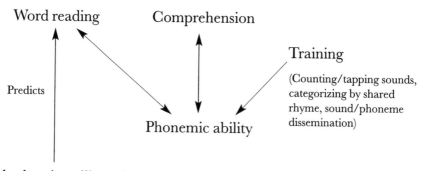

Figure 9.2 Phonological knowledge and literacy.

The ability to blend sounds together or to segment or separate sound units, and the use of alliteration and rhyming skills are all good predictors of later reading skills. Phonemic ability, which again is associated with the relationship between speech and the sound, and also syllabification skills, sounding out words, separating them into sound units, are also important for word reading. There is an interaction here, i.e. the better you are at reading, the better you are at phonemic skills. Conversely, the better you are at phonemic skills the better your reading is likely to be. This interrelationship is, of course, one of the problems in aspects of dyslexia research, particularly when looking at control groups. Phonemic ability, which to some extent is interactive, dependent on and gives rise to good word reading, is also linked to comprehension. Training, i.e. teaching by categorizing sounds, phoneme discrimination and other such skills, can improve phonemic ability which underlies both word reading and comprehension; this in turn can give rise to improved phonemic ability. It sounds rather complex and full of circularities, but it is important to understand this interactivity and 'networking' of the learning process.

Research suggests that, if a child has good skills in the area that predicts reading shown in Figure 9.1 at age 4 or 5 years, he or she will become a good reader at 6 or 7 years, and a number of longitudinal studies have supported this (e.g. Bryant and Bradley, 1985). However, there is a two-way relationship between word reading and phonemic ability. As we develop our reading skills, e.g. alphabetical skills, we would expect phonemic abilities to develop, particularly those in letter–sound or grapheme–phoneme correspondence; if we look at Frith's premise that early alphabetical skills derive from spelling, the notion of mapping letters on to their sound units is also a phonemic ability relating to reading. We thus have the problem that an individual who shows poor phonemic abilities may show those resulting from their poor reading skills, rather than poor reading being caused by poor phonemic ability. There is also a relationship between phonemic abilities and comprehension. Obviously, the better you are reading, the more your comprehension skills will develop; there is also the relationship between specific training of phonemic ability skills which will develop phonemic ability. We therefore have at least three different aspects – word reading, comprehension and specific teaching – that will develop phonological abilities. (Note that the term phonological skills or phonemic ability is used very widely here and the reader is referred to Tables 3.2 and 7.7 for a description for some of these subskills.)

This interrelationship between cognitive skills, as measured in the laboratory or by psychometrics, and the reading, writing and spelling process is a problematic one. Let us take, for example, a typically early experiment looking at the ability of children to blend sounds together. The

test, i.e. dependent variable, might be the score out of 10 for a child's ability to put /c/–/a/–/t/ together to make a word along with nine other
examples. Table 9.1 shows typical control groups that might be used.

Table 9.1 Control groups used in a hypothetical study

	Chronological age (years)	Reading age (years)
Dyslexic children	10	7
Control group 1	10	10
Control group 2	7	7

   One method of examining the relationship between sound blending and
dyslexia would be using children with dyslexia and control group 1. Typically, the dyslexic children might have an average chronological age of 10
and be reading 3 years behind with an average reading age of 7. However, a
control group would be reading at their chronological age. If, for example,
the dyslexics were found to be weaker at sound blending than the controls,
one could say that sound-blending difficulties are a cause of dyslexia.
However, we could argue that the sound-blending difficulties of children
with dyslexia are not a result of the underlying phonological deficit or
'dyslexia', but a result of their reading ability. Perhaps the skills of reading
from the level of a 7-year-old through to the level of a 10-year-old require
more phonemic awareness and alphabetical skills, which develop sound
blending. An analogy might be the skill of swimming. If we took a group of
good, highly trained swimmers and a group of non-swimmers, we might
find that the trained swimmers would have larger pectoral muscles. We
could conclude that having large pectoral muscles meant that you became a
good swimmer. However, a much more likely explanation is that, as you
learn to swim, become a better swimmer and train often, so your pectoral
muscles develop. Having large pectoral muscles is a result of swimming.
Thus good sound blending could be a result of better reading.
   In an attempt to sort out this chicken and egg argument, most recent
research looking at aspects of cognitive development that are linked to
reading and spelling development uses a similar control group to control
group 2 shown in Table 9.1. Here we have children who are at the same
reading level as children with dyslexia – they, of course, need to be
younger children so that they are 'normal' and do not have reading and
spelling difficulties. However, this means that, if you find that the younger
control group who are reading at the same level as the older children with
dyslexia are better, in this example, at sound blending, we can be more
confident about the assertion that weak sound-blending ability in dyslexic
children shows a causal relationship to their weakness in reading. This is

the result of the fact that, despite having the same reading level as non-dyslexic children, they have a weaker sound-blending ability. Of course there are also difficulties in interpretation. The fact is that the control group are developmentally younger, and making generalizations comparing this with an older group may be fraught with difficulties. Furthermore, some researchers argue that the very point is that the children with dyslexia, despite being exposed to the same teaching experience and reading material as other children, are not acquiring reading and spelling (and sound-blending skills) and this itself is of significant interest.

As we can see, these issues are complex; heated debates occur at scientific conferences, with people taking particular views. Fortunately, with my teacher's, as opposed to my psychologist's, hat on I can say that it will not affect very much how I actually teach the children; I am interested in results rather than the underlying theory. The theory does guide the way that I teach and the principles I use. However, the specific features of a child, which I have gleaned from assessment and observed in my teaching, are probably more important in guiding the detail of my teaching. What is quite clear to me is that children with dyslexia show a wide variety of different behaviours under the general umbrella of the syndrome of dyslexia, which would include aspects of visual processing, motor development and other approaches that we examined in earlier chapters.

To return to the phonological deficit notion, however, it is worth commenting that this has become a central plank for many researchers, almost to the level that it has become an accepted assumption that children with dyslexia have phonological weaknesses. Part of the Orton Society's definition of dyslexia reads '... characterized by difficulties in single word decoding, usually reflecting insufficient phonological processing abilities'. The implication is that the main weakness of a person with dyslexia will be with phonological processing abilities, resulting in single word decoding problems.

We can be more specific about the phonological weaknesses shown by children with dyslexia. The reader might want to refer to Table 3.3 (p. 45) for different skills tapped under 'phonological' and Table 7.7 (p. 109) for general comments on phonological development and dyslexia. However, Table 9.2 summarizes some specific research findings. (See also an earlier review by Snowling, 1987, 2000.)

The results expressed in Table 9.2 (p. 126) can be subsumed under the notion that children with dyslexia are weak at the explicit analysis of phonemic or perhaps acoustic information needed for accurate reading and spelling, and the notion of 'fuzzy representations' has been put forward by those examining the relationship between speech development and written language development. Basically, the idea is that poorly specified phonological representations prevent the precise learning of phoneme– grapheme

Table 9.2 Examples of studies on phonological deficits in dyslexia

Findings	Examples of researchers
Weak sound blending good predictor of dyslexia (poor phonemic awareness/segmentation skills). Also found weak auditory and visual short-term memory good predictors	Newton and Thomson (1976)
Dyslexic children weaker at naming tasks, e.g. pictures, colours, letters. As good as controls for visual recognition itself (poor phonological/verbal coding)	Denckla and Rudel (1976) Liberman et al. (1977) Ellis and Miles (1978) Swan and Goswami (1997
Dyslexic children weaker reading and repeating non-words (poor phonological representation/sublexical components)	Snowling (1981) Bruck and Treiman (1998) Castles and Coltheart (1993)
At-risk (for reading) children weaker on vocabulary, phonological awareness, letter knowledge	Scarborough (1990) Snowling and Nation (1997)
Poor rhyming and alliteration are good predictors of later reading failure (poor sound categorization skills)	Bradley and Bryant (1983)
Brain imaging differential activation of left hemisphere in phonological tasks in dyslexics	Paulesu et al. (1996) Shaywitz et al. (1998)
Weak phonological segmentation (and naming/short-term memory)	Ellis and Large (1988)
Dyslexic children weaker on word generating on the basis of phoneme, but equal on categories (weak alphabetical skills)	Frith, Lauder and Frith (1995)
Dyslexic children weak on grapheme/phoneme tasks, specifically on sound coding. Good on visual coding	Mark et al. (1977) Snowling (1980) Hick (1981)
Dyslexic children poor at segmenting syllables into phonemes	Fox and Routh (1980)

mapping. In other words, if you cannot follow speech sounds very well, this prevents you from relating that particular sound to the particular letter combinations representing that sound. Obviously the difficulties in phonemic mapping, i.e. which particular aspects of the sounds are represented by which particular part of the word, are implicated here; the reader may remember that this could be at the phonemic level, e.g. f-r-o-g, onset and rime line, e.g. fr-og or syllable level, e.g. mag-net.

All of these have been suggested as being weak at one point or another in children with dyslexia and, if there are no stable representations of these elements, there will be no sublexical developments. This implies that there will be no ability to build up parts of words and therefore no generalization to new words using alphabetical skills, in learning new words to read. We have therefore some quite strong evidence that phonological processing skills are certainly intimately tied up with dyslexic learning difficulties. We have already seen that recent neuropsychological evidence in (see Chapter

6) highlights the speech-to-phonemic awareness to written language link as being weak in people with dyslexia. One suggestion is that, although the 'normal' brain is processing one sound at a time, people perceive/combine the letters as a whole word. In good readers, this process is so fast that, although they read whole words, in fact they are converting letters on the written page to sounds. Therefore, to read the word 'cat' the reader initially must parse, or segment, the word into its underlying phonological elements. Once the word is in its phonological form, it can be identified and understood. In dyslexia, an inefficient phonological module produces representations that are less clear and hence difficult to bring into awareness. Neuropsychologically, letter identification will be activated in the extrastriate cortex in the occipital lobe for both dyslexic and 'normal' readers; however, phonological processing will activate the inferior temporal gyrus (Broca's area) only in 'normal' readers.

There are, however, a number of question marks about the full acceptance of a phonological deficit as a total explanation of dyslexia. The first of these is what one might term the 'syndrome of dyslexia', i.e. examining what dyslexic children actually do. One of the key features is that many dyslexics have problems with is organization. One might almost argue that weak organizational skills underlie many problems of children with dyslexia, including things that we might describe as being concerned with short-term memory, e.g. remembering instructions and events during the day, as well as longer verbal memory tasks, such as days of the week, months of the year and tables. Some children with dyslexia have problems in motor development (see Chapter 6), and others have apparent visual difficulties (see also Chapter 6). So, we cannot just accept phonological deficit as the only answer because there are other models and theories of aetiology.

A second problem is the extent of the phonological weakness and why it does not extend to other aspects of language. Many dyslexics with dyslexia have very good speaking and comprehension skills, whether measured psychometrically or by talking to dyslexic children. In reading itself, a good deal of research (see Thomson, 1990) shows that dyslexic children are much better at comprehension skills; indeed Stanovich (1994) argues that one condition of dyslexia could be the discrepancy between word reading and comprehension skills (see Chapter 4). If we accept that specific phonological skills may be weak in children with dyslexia, surely that would affect other aspects of verbal reasoning, vocabulary development, etc. Phonological weakness could affect the metacognitive, i.e. the conscious segmentation of alphabet, or what Galaburda (1999) elegantly calls 'parsing the phonetic stream'. Another problem is the relationship between phonological deficits and intelligence. We have examined this in relation to discrepancy models in Chapter 4, but if we look at Figure 9.3, taken from Frith (1999), we can see another proposed relationship between tests that tap grapheme–phoneme (G–P) knowledge, phonological processes and so-called 'g' or general ability.

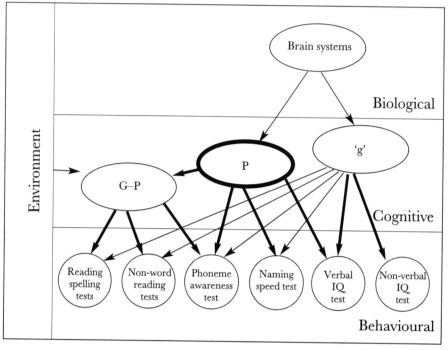

Figure 9.3 Relationship between grapheme–phoneme knowledge (G–P) , phonological process (P) and general ability ('g'). From Frith (1999) Paradoxes in Developmental Dyslexia. John Wiley and Sons. Reproduced with permission.

One problem here is that weak phonological processing can give rise to problems in the Verbal IQ, as well as grapheme–phoneme knowledge and other behavioural skills. However, children with dyslexia do not in general have a weaker Verbal than Non-Verbal IQ. If Verbal IQ is lower on the Wechsler Intelligence Test for Children, it is often the result of Information, Arithmetic and Digit Span being weak. Of the 'ACID' profile (see page 37) two (three if Digit Span is used to compute IQ) subtests on the Verbal Scale are relatively poor compared with just one (Coding) on the Performance Scale. Thus any Verbal/Performance discrepancy may be caused by subtest differences, not the general IQ.

Another problem is that, if G–P knowledge is linked to environment, i.e. teaching methods, then specific weaknesses in these areas will be very much affected by received teaching. Some of the research I have undertaken with students at East Court has shown that dyslexic children given help in their reading, writing and spelling also develop their phonological skills. Using the Phonological Abilities Battery (see Chapter 3), it was found that dyslexic children who had made good progress in reading performed well on the test. Basically, if one assumes that phonological abilities are causal, one would expect them still to remain weak even though children's reading, writing and spelling develop, so we come back to cause-and-effect interpretations.

A third problem is the overlap and direction of explanation of phonological deficits and short-term memory. There have been a number of attempts to claim that phonological deficits are a core feature and therefore we can reject the notions of short-term memory weaknesses. This has been the result of differences between the notion of 'short-term memory' and 'working memory'. The latter enables a more detailed analysis of the processes involved (see Chapter 8). I believe that there is really not much distinction between the phonological loop in working memory and phonological deficits. These seem to be all part of the same weak process in people with dyslexia; the next section looks in more detail at research into memory and dyslexia.

Memory difficulties in dyslexia

As well as phonological process, there is also a long history of research into memory difficulties in dyslexia. Table 9.3 summarizes examples of these. Some of the results can clearly be interpreted as phonological or verbal

Table 9.3 Examples of studies on dyslexia and memory

Poor performance on 'span' or capacity tasks (weaker information processing)	Bakker (1972) Miles and Ellis (1981) Naidoo (1972) Thomson and Wilsher (1979) Cohen and Netley (1981)
Memory for verbal tasks weaker (poor verbal coding)	Vellutino (1979), Vellutino et al. (1975) Shankweiler et al. (1979) Mann, Liberman and Shankweiler (1980) Jorm (1979) Rack J (1985)
Weak short-term memory, normal long-term memory (early coding problems in memory)	Nelson and Warrington (1980) Jorm (1979) Vellutino et al. (1975)
Sequential memory (weak sequencing skills)	Thomson and Newton (1979) Zurif and Carson (1970) Bakker (1972); Bakker and Schroots (1981) Thomson (1977)

coding, but others seem to suggest other factors in memory. Specific phonemic skills include: remembering phoneme–grapheme correspondence rules in order to produce the correct output of letters in spelling; remembering letter-by-letter sounds; remembering sounds long enough to blend these in forming words (e.g. c-a-t = cat); being able to correct spelling errors by remembering what the whole word or letter combination looks; being able to copy spellings from the blackboard without having constantly to look up every 2 seconds or so; and maintaining an auditory or visual image of a spelling or reading pattern long enough for it to be internalised and transferred into other memory systems.

If we look specifically at the proposed working memory system outlined in Chapter 8, we see that the skills described in our models of reading and spelling process are part of the phonological loop. Thus, speech-to-reading difficulties are accounted for by problems in the articulating control system and grapheme–phoneme correspondence problems by the phonological store. In addition, the 'inner voice' or articulatory control system is a serial and temporal system that might account for the sequencing and capacity findings outlined above.

We can build up more explicit links to the alphabet weaknesses proposed as the core phonological deficit. To build up their vocabulary and read new words, children typically begin to exploit an alphabetical strategy. This approach facilitates the decoding of unfamiliar letter sequences by applying the associations between letters and their sounds. Forming long-term representations of novel phonological material is a key component of written language development, especially at the alphabetical stage, e.g. Gathercole and Baddeley (1989) state that 'phonological memory appears to make a critical contribution to reading development at the point at which relationships between letter groups and sounds are being acquired'. It seems that it is the phonological loop component of 'working memory' that facilitates the learning of new words. They view this ability to generate long-lasting representations of brief and novel speech events as a fundamental human capacity, and believe that it is this predisposition for vocabulary development that provides the basis for literacy. Indeed, the successful building of an internal store of words, or lexicon, is thought by some to be the main determinant of a child's eventual educational attainment (Sternberg, 1987). Baddeley, Gathercole and Papagno (1998) cite a number of studies that have found that performance on verbal short-term memory tasks, subserved by the phonological loop, correlates with good vocabulary knowledge (e.g. Gathercole and Adams, 1993; Michas and Henry, 1994). According to Gathercole and Baddeley (1989), the function of the phonological loop is to provide temporary storage of novel phonological stimuli while more permanent memory representations are being formed. In their view, some children have a memory deficit that reflects an impairment in the ability to store phonological material in 'working memory', thus interfering with the acquisition of long-term phonological memories. The exact nature of this impairment, they think, has still to be determined but they put forward a number of possibilities, e.g. a 'noisy' system could result in phonological traces being less easily discriminated at retrieval. Alternatively, the capacity to store brief phonological representations may be less in these individuals, leading to fewer items being stored or items being inadequately represented. Another possibility is that the phonological trace decays more rapidly in people with dyslexia.

So, there are very specific parallels between phonological skills in general and working memory models. However, if we look at other aspects of the memory models, we find some useful pointers on other aspects of dyslexia, e.g. attentional focus problems. The 'but I taught you this yesterday' and the 'but didn't you hear me say page 8–10 for your homework' and similar comments could be part of the phonological loop, but does have 'central executive' implications (see Chapter 8)

The central executive has a number of functions including the following:

- Strategy
- Monitoring and planning
- Attentional control
- Initiation, sustaining, shifting, inhibition, stopping.

Attention is by its nature selective, whether to an internal event, such as an image of a spelling pattern, or external to a teacher, classmate, worksheet or blackboard. The direction and focus of attention are thus selective and will involve attention shifting. Thus, the sequence of events attended to and the process of 'engage'/'disengage' are all elements of the central executive. A further element of attention is accuracy over an extended period of time, i.e. sustained attention.

The reader who is experienced in working with children with dyslexia will note the resonance of these features. Many dyslexic children with dyslexia find it difficult to keep engaged and will often switch focus. The maintenance of attention, particularly to written language that is difficult for them, is also problematic. (How often do we as adults keep our focus on something that we find difficult?)

There has been little work on examining the role of the central executive in children with dyslexia, but what we can say is that the problems in phonology, written language and attention are all elements of working memory systems. Individual differences in working memory organization explains specific dyslexic features (e.g. digit span, lack of attention to enable encoding into phonological loop space), as well as the phonological deficits that are more directly related to written language systems.

However, all of this is still the subject of ongoing research and I am afraid I still cannot say to the reader 'this is the proven cause of dyslexia'. It is a syndrome of related difficulties. As we have seen, core elements are differential processing of phonological material in the left hemisphere. This gives rise to the core phonological/working memory deficits at a cognitive level. However, we still need to take into account the motor and visual systems mentioned in Chapter 6. All of these points have been discussed in earlier chapters.

The final comment really is a slightly tongue in cheek one, because I feel that there is a great deal of what one might term 'academic jargon' in relation to phonological deficit. Some of the early researchers talked about specific weaknesses in grapheme–phoneme correspondence. This is nothing less than saying that children with dyslexia have problems in learning letter–sound links, hardly a revelation and really a description of their difficulties! Table 9.4 shows some descriptions by research

Table 9.4 Research and teaching-oriented approaches to specific learning difficulties

Research psychologist	Experienced teacher
Difficulties with:	
Grapheme–phoneme links	Problems learning the letters of the alphabet
Grapheme–phoneme conversion rules	Weak decoding skills
Grapheme–phoneme mapping	Forgets which letter(s) to use for the sound
Phonemic awareness	Confuses sounds in words
Systematic simplifications of vowels	Confuses vowel sounds in words
Metaphonological skills	Problems in following speech and applying to spelling
Visual orthographic processing	Weak proofreading – problems remembering what a word looks like
Phonological coding	Problems with phonics (yes, but specifically where?)
Phonological segmentation skills	Can't beat out syllables in words
Phonological recombination skills	Can't blend sounds
Lexical access	Can't remember whole word spelling or meaning
Teach by:	
Visualization of orthographic patterns	Look and say
Explicit phoneme–grapheme mapping	Phonics
Lexical analogy	Word families
Multisensory simultaneous oral spelling	Hearing, saying letters, writing or tracing, saying, reading
Orthographic conventions	Spelling rules
Onset and rime	Split words into consonant blend unit plus vowel/consonant unit
Systematic simplification of phonological segmentation process	Syllable analysis

psychologists against those of teachers, and various other ways of describing processes. These might help the reader to 'decode the jargon'!

Further reading

Hulme C, Snowling MJ (1994) *Reading Development and Dyslexia*. London: Whurr, Chapter 1–6.

Miles TR, Miles E (1999) *Dyslexia or Hundred Years on*. Milton Keynes: Open University Press, Chapter 4–7.

Pumfrey P, Reason R (1991) *Specific Learning Difficulties*. Windsor: NFER–Nelson, Chapter 5

Snowling MJ (1987, 2000) *Dyslexia: A cognitive development perspective*. Oxford: Blackwell.

Snowling MJ, Stackhouse J (1996) *Dyslexia, Speech and Language*. London: Whurr, Chapters 3 and 4.

Thomson ME (1990) *Developmental Dyslexia*. London: Whurr, Chapter 3.

Appendix: Tests

The following are examples of tests under four headings of 'Ability', 'Attainment', 'Diagnostic' and 'Screening'. Three reflect the categories of assessments from Chapter 3 but I have also included examples of screening tests for dyslexia as a separate category. Some of these also include ability, attainment and diagnostic sections. I have made some comments where appropriate. It is not an exhaustive list and readers will find many more examples of Ability and Attainment tests in the NFER–Nelson and Psychological Corporation brochures and reviewed in, for example, Reid (1998) (see Chapter 3, Further reading).

Note that the Wechsler and British Ability Scales are available only for to Psychologists with specific training.

Ability tests

Dunn LM, Dunn LM, Whetton C, Burley J (1997) *British Picture Vocabulary Scale*, 2nd edn (BPVS-II). Windsor: NFER–Nelson,.
A measure of receptive vocabulary across a wide age range.

Elliott CD, Smith P, McCulloch K (1996) *British Ability Scales*, 2nd edn (BAS II). Windsor: NFER–Nelson.
Individually given intelligence test.

Naglieri JA (1985) *Matrix Analogies Test* (MAT). London: Harcourt, The Psychological Corporation.
Naglieri JA (1996) *Naglieri Nonverbal Ability Test* (NNAT). London: Harcourt, The Psychological Corporation.
Raven J (1972) *Raven's Progressive Matrices*. Windsor: NFER–Nelson.
Raven J (1995) *Raven's Progressive Matrices Standard and Coloured*, 2nd edn. Windsor: NFER–Nelson.

Raven J (1998) *Raven's Progressive Matrices*, 3rd edn. Windsor: NFER–Nelson.
All of the above tests are measures of visuospatial reasoning.

Wechsler D (1992) *Wechsler Intelligence Scale For Children*, 3rd edn (WISC-III). London: Harcourt, The Psychological Corporation.
Individually given intelligence test.

Attainment tests

Neale MD (1997) *Neale Analysis of Reading Ability*, revised (NARA-II; second revised British edn. Standardization by Whetton C, Caspall L, McCulloch K). Windsor: NFER–Nelson.
Prose reading giving Accuracy, Rate (speed) and Comprehension (questions on text after it has been read) scores.

Peters ML, Smith B (1990) *Spelling in Context*. Windsor: NFER–Nelson.
Passages for dictation.

Rust J, Golombok S, Trickey G (1993) *WORD: Wechsler Objective Reading Dimension*. London: Harcourt, The Psychological Corporation.
Three attainment tests: Basic Reading (individual word reading), Spelling (graded individual words) and Reading Comprehension (graded texts with questions).

Vernon M (1976) *Vernon Graded Word Spelling Test*. London: Hodder & Stoughton
Graded individual word spelling.

Vincent D, Claydon J (1982) *Diagnostic Spelling Test*. Windsor: NFER–Nelson.
Vincent D, de la Mare M (1990) *Individual Reading Analysis*. Windsor: NFER–Nelson.
Prose reading.

Wilkinson GS (1993) *The Wide Range Achievement Test*, 3rd edn (WRAT-3). London: Harcourt, The Psychological Corporation.
Test of graded individual word reading and spelling (also arithmetic).

Diagnostic tests

Frederickson N, Frith U, Reason R (1997) *Phonological Assessment Battery* (PhAB). Windsor: NFER–Nelson.
A number of phonological tests including non-word reading, rhyming, spoonerisms, etc.

Snowling MJ, Stothard SE, Maclean J (1996) *Graded Non-word Reading Test.* Bury St Edmunds: Thames Valley Trust Co.
Graded individual non-word reading test.

Muter V, Hulme C, Snowling M (1997) *Phonological Abilities Test.* London: Harcourt, The Psychological Corporation.
Similar to the PhAB but for younger children.

Screening tests

Fawcett A, Nicholson R (1997 onwards) *Dyslexia Screening Tests* (DEST, DST, DAST). London: Harcourt, Psychological Corporation.
Screening for pre-school, child and adult. Phonological items as well as motor development.

Miles TR (1983) *The Bangor Dyslexia Test.* Wisbech: Learning Development Aids/Living and Learning.
Criterion-oriented screen for dyslexia.

Newton M, Thomson ME (1976) *The Aston Index*. Wisbech: Learning Development Aids/Living and Learning.
Ability measures including a vocabulary scale, attainments (Schonell Graded Word Reading and Spelling) and diagnostic items such as Digit Span, Sound Blending, etc.

References

Adams MJ (1996) *Beginning to Read, Thinking and Learning about Print*. Cambridge, MA: MIT Press.

Annett M (1991) Laterality and cerebral dominance. *J Child Psychol Psychiatry* **32**: 219–32.

Baddeley A, Gathercole S, Papagno C (1998). The phonological loop as a language learning device. *Psychol Rev* **105**(1).

Bakker DJ (1972) Temporal order in normal and disturbed reading. *Developmental and Neuropsychological Aspects in Normal and Reading-retarded Children*. Rotterdam: Rotterdam University Press.

Bakker DJ, Schroots HJ (1981) Temporal order in normal and disturbed reading. In: Pavlides G, Miles T, eds, *Dyslexia Research and its Applications to Education*. Chichester: John Wiley.

Bakwin H (1973) Reading disability in twins. *Dev Med Child Neurol* **15**: 184–7.

Beaumont JG, Thomson ME, Rugg M (1981) An intrahemispheric integration deficit in dyslexia. *Curr Psychol Res* **1**: 185–9.

Bradley L, Bryant, PE (1983) Categorising sounds and learning to read – a causal connection. *Nature* **301**: 419–21.

British Psychological Society (1999) Working Party of Division of Educational and Child Psychology of the BPS. *Dyslexia, Literacy and Psychological Assessment*. Leicester: BPS.

Bruck M, Treiman R (1998) Phonological awareness and spelling in normal children and dyslexics; The care of initial consonant clusters. *J Exp Child Psychol* **50**: 156–78.

Bryant P, Bradley L (1985) *Children's Reading Problems*. Oxford: Blackwell.

Cardon LR, DeFries JC, Fulker DW, Kimberling WJ, Pennington BF, Smith SD (1994) Quantitative trait locus for reading disability on chromosome 6. *Science* **265**: 276–9.

Castles A, Coltheart M (1993) Varieties of developmental dyslexia. *Cognition* **47**: 149–80.

Cohen RL, Netley C (1981) Short term memory deficits in reading disabled children, in the absence of opportunity for rehearsal strategies. *Intelligence* **5**: 69–76.

Coltheart M, Jackson NE (1998) Forum on dyslexia. *Child Psychol Psychiatry Rev* 3(1): 12–16.

Conners CK (1970) Cortical Visual evoked response in children with learning disorders. *Psychophysiology* **7**: 418–78

Connors CK, Bouin AG, Winglee M, Louge L, O'Donnell D, Smith A (1984) Piracetum and event-related potentials in dyslexic children. *Psychopharmacol Bull* **20**: 667–73.

DeFries JC (1985) Colorado reading project. In: Gray DB, Kavanagh JF, eds, *Biobehavioural Measures of Dyslexia*. Parkton, MD: York Press, pages 107–22.

DeFries JC (1991) Genetics and dyslexia: an overview. In: Snowling MJ, Thomson ME, eds, *Dyslexia: Integrating theory and practice*. London: Whurr Publishers: pages .

DeFries JC, Decker SN (1982) Genetic aspects of reading disability: The Colorado Family Reading Study. In: Malatesha RN, Aaron PG, eds, *Reading Disability: Varieties and treatments*. New York: Academic Press, pp. 255–79.

DeFries JC, Gillis JJ, Wadsworth SJ (1990) Genes and genders: A twin study of reading disability. In: Galaburda AM, ed. *The Extraordinary Brain: Neurobiologic issues in developmental dyslexia,*. Cambridge, MA: MIT Press.

Denckla MB, Rudel R (1976) Naming of pictured objects by dyslexic and other learning disabled children. *Brain Language* **3**: 1–15.

Dunn LIM, Dunn LM, Whetton C, Burley J (1997) *British Picture Vocabulary Scale*, 2nd edn (BPVS-II) Windsor, Berks: NFER–Nelson.

Ehri L (1991) The development of reading and spelling in children; an overview in Snowling M, Thomson ME., eds, *Dyslexia: Integrating theory and practice*. London: Whurr Publishers.

Eisenberg L (1966) The epidemiology of reading retardation and a program for preventive intervention. In: Money J, ed., *The Disabled Reader: Education of the Dyslexic Child*. Baltimore, MD: Johns Hopkins University Press.

Ellis N, Large B (1988) The early stages of reading: A longitudinal study. *Applied Cogn Psychol* **2**: 47–76.

Ellis N, Miles T (1978) Visual information processing in dyslexic children. In: Gruneberg M, Morris P, Sykes R, eds, *Practical Aspects of Memory*. London: Academic Press.

Finucci JM, Guthrie JT, Childs AL, Abbey H, Childs B (1976) The genetics of specific reading disability. *Ann Human Genet* **40**: 1–23.

Fisher SE, Marlow AJ, Lamb J (1999) A quantitative-trait locus on chromosome 6p influence different aspects of developmental dyslexia. *Am J Human Genet* **64**: 146–56.

Fox B, Routh D (1980) Phonemic analysis and reading disability in children. *J Psycholinguis Res* **9**(2): 115–19.

Frederickson N, Frith U, Reason R (1997) *Phonological Assessment Battery (PhAB)* Windsor, Berkshire: NFER–Nelson.

Frith U (1985) Beneath the surface of developmental dyslexia. In: Marshall JC, Patterson KE, Colheart M, eds, *Surface Dyslexia in Adults and Children*, London: Routledge & Kegan Paul.

Frith U (1992) Model for developmental disorders. *Psychologist* BPS Jan.

Frith U (1999) Paradoxes in the definition of dyslexia. *Dyslexia* 5: 4: 192–215.

Frith U, Landerl K, Frith C (1995) Dyslexia and verbal fluency: more evidence for a phonological deficit. *Dyslexia* **1**: 2–11.

Galaburda AM (1989) Ordinary and extraordinary brain development. Anatomical variation in developmental dyslexia. *Ann Dyslexia* **39**: 67–80.

Galaburda AM (1999) Developmental dyslexia: A multi-level syndrome. *Dyslexia* 5(4): 183–91.

Galaburda AM, Signoret JC, Ronthal M (1985) Left posterior angiomatous anomaly and developmental dyslexia: report of five cases. *Neurology* **35**(suppl): 198.

Gathercole SE, Adams A (1993) Phonological working memory in very young children. *Dev Psychol* **29**: 770–8.

Gathercole SE, Baddeley AD (1989) Evaluation of the role of phonological STM in the development of vocabulary in children: a longitudinal study. *J Memory Lang* 28, 200–13.

Gayan J, Smith SD, Cherny SS, Cardon LR (1999) Quantitative trait locus for specific language and reading deficits on chromosome 6p. *Am J Human Genet* **64**: 157–64.

Goswami U (1986) Children's use of analogy in learning to read: a developmental study. *J Exp Child Psychol* **42**: 72–83.

Goswami U (1988) Children's use of analogy in learning to spell. *Br J Dev Psychol* **6**: 21–33.

Goswami U, Bryant P (1990) *Phonological Skills and Learning to Read*. Hove, Sussex: Erlbaum.

Grigorenko EL, Wood FB, Meyer MS, Hart LA, Speed WC, Shuster A, Pauls DL (1997) Susceptibility loci for distinct components of developmental dyslexia on chromosome 6 and 15. *Am J Human Genet* **60**: 27–39.

Hallgren B (1950) Specific dyslexia ('congenital word blindness'): A clinical and genetic study. *Acta Psychiatr Neurol Scand Suppl* 65.

Hedderly RG (1995) The assessment of SpLD pupils for examination arrangements. *Dyslexia Rev* **7**(2): 12–16

Henderson EH (1981) *Teaching Children to Read and Spell.* Chicago, IL: Northern Illinois Press.

Hick C (1981) B/D confusions in dyslexia. *J Res Reading* **4**: 21–28.

Hinshelwood J (1900) Congenital word blindness. *Lancet* **i**: 1506–8.

Jorm AF (1979) The cognitive and neurological basis of developmental dyslexia: a theoretical framework and review. *Cognition* **7**: 19–33.

Liberman IY, Shankweiler D, Liberman AM, Fowler C, Fischer FW (1977) Phonetic segmentation and recoding in the beginning reader. In: Reber AS, Scarborough D, eds, *Towards a Psychology of Reading. The Proceedings of the CUNY Conferences.* Hillsdale, NJ: Lawrence Erlbaum Associates.

Mann VA, Liberman IY, Shankweiler D (1980) Children's memory for sentences and word strings in relation to reading ability. *Memory Cognition* **8**: 329–35.

Mark LS, Shankweiler D, Liberman IY, Fowler CA (1977) Phonetic recoding and reading difficulty in beginning readers. *Memory Cognition* **5**: 623–9.

Marsh G, Friedman M, Welch V, Desbery P (1981) A cognitive developmental theory of reading acquisition. In: Mackinson GE, Waller TG, eds, *Reading Records: Advancing in theory and practice*, Vol. 3, New York: Academic Press, pages 199–221.

Michas IC, Henry LA (1994) The link between phonological memory and vocabulary acquisition. *Br J Dev Psychol* **12**: 147–63.

Miles T (1974) *Understanding Dyslexia*, London: Priory Press.

Miles T, Ellis N (1981) A lexical encoding deficiency 1 and 11. Experimental evidence and classical observations. In: Pavlidis G, Miles T, eds, *Dyslexia Research and its Application to Education.* Chichester: Wiley.

Morgan WP (1896) A case of congenital word blindness. *British Medical Journal* **ii**: 378.

Muter V (1997) Phonological assessment of dyslexics. Workshop/paper at BDA Conference, York.

Naglieri JA (1985) *Matrix Analogies Test (Short Form)* Columbus, OH: Charles Merrill.

Naidoo S (1972) *Specific Dyslexia.* London: Pitman.

Neale MD (1997) *Neale Analysis of Reading Ability – Revised* (NARA-II; second revised British edn) Windsor: NFER–Nelson

Nelson HE, Warrington EK (1980) An investigation of memory functions in dyslexic children. *Br J Psychol* **71**: 487–503.

Newton M (1970) A neuro-psychological investigation into dyslexia. In: Franklin AW, Naidoo S, eds, *Assessment and Teaching of Dyslexia in Children.* London: ICAP.

Newton MJ, Thomson ME (1976) *The Aston Index: A screening procedure for written language difficulties.* Wisbech: Learning Development Aids.

Nicholson RI, Fawcett AJ (1999) Developmental dyslexia. The role of the cerebellum. *Dyslexia* **5**(3): 53–177.

Orton ST (1937) *Reading, Writing and Speech Problems in Children.* London: Chapman & Hall.

Owen FW (1979) Dyslexia – genetic aspects. In: Benton AL, Pearl D, eds, *Dyslexia: An appraisal of current knowledge.* New York: Oxford University Press.

Owen FW, Adams PA, Forrest T, Stoltz LM, Fisher S (1971) Learning disorders in children: Sibling studies. *Monographs of the Society for Research in Child Development*, Vol. 36. Chicago, IL: University of Chicago Press.

Paulesu E, Frith U, Snowling M, Gallagher A, Morton J, Frackowiak RSJ, Frith CD (1996) Is developmental dyslexia a disconnection syndrome? Evidence from PET scanning. *Brain* **119**: 143–57.

Pavlides GTH (1981) Sequencing, eye movements and the early objective diagnosis of dyslexia. In: Pavlides GTH, Miles T, eds, *Dyslexia: Research and its Applications to Dyslexia.* Chichester: Wiley.

Pennington BF (1999) Toward an integrated understanding of dyslexia: Genetic, neurological, and cognitive mechanisms. *Dev Psychopathol* **11**: 629–54.

Rack J (1985) Orthographic and phonetic encoding in normal and dyslexic readers. *Br J Psychol* **76**: 325–40.

Rutter M, Tizard J, Whitmore K (1970) *Education, Health and Behaviour*. London: Longman.

Scarborough HS (1990) Very early language deficits in dyslexic children. *Child Dev* **61**: 1728–43.

Seidenberg M, McClelland J (1989) A distributed, developmental model of word recognition and naming. *Psychol Rev* **96**: 523–68

Shankweiler D, Libermann IY, Mark LS, Fowler CA, Fischer FW (1979) The speech code and learning to read. *J Exp Psychol Human Learning Memory* **5**: 531–45.

Shaywitz SE, Shaywitz BA, Pugh KR (1998) Functional disruption in the organisation of the brain for reading in dyslexia. *Proc Natl Acad Sci* **95**: 2636–41.

Siegal LS (1989) IQ is irrelevant to the definition of learning disabilities. *J Learning Disabilities* **22**: 469–78, 486.

Sladen BK (1971) Inheritance of dyslexia. *Bull Orton Society* **31**: 30–9.

Smith SD, Kimberling WJ, Pennington BA, Lubs HA (1982) Specific reading disability: Identification of an inherited form through linkage analysis. *Science* **219**: 1345–7.

Snowling MJ (1980) The development of grapheme-phoneme correspondences in normal and dyslexic readers. *J Exp Child Psychol* **29**: 294–305.

Snowling MJ (1981) Phonemic deficits in developmental dyslexia. *Psychol Res* **43**: 219–35.

Snowling MJ (1987) *Dyslexia: A cognitive developmental perspective*. Oxford, Blackwell.

Snowling M (1998) Dyslexia as a phonological deficit: Evidence and implications. *Child Psychol Psychiatry Rev* **3**(1): 4–11.

Snowling MJ, Nation KA (1997) Language, phonology and learning to read. In: Hulme C, Snowling M, eds, *Dyslexia: Biology, cognition and intervention*. London: Whurr Publishers.

Snowling MJ, Stothard SE, Maclean J (1996) *Graded Nonword Reading Test*. Bury St Edmunds: Thames Valley Trust Co.

Stanovich KE (1994) Annotation: does dyslexia exist? *J Child Psychol Psychiatry* **35**: 579–95.

Stein J, Fowler S (1985) Effects of monocular occlusion on visuomotor perception and reading in dyslexic children. *The Lancet* **2**(8446): 69–73.

Stein J, Talcott J (1999) Impaired neuronal timing in developmental dyslexia – The magnocellular hypothesis. *Dyslexia* **5**(2): 59–77.

Sternberg R (1987) Most vocabulary is learned from context. In: McKeown M, Curtis M, eds, *The Nature of Vocabulary Acquisition*. Hillsdale, NJ: Lawrence Erlbaum Associates Inc., pp. 89–106.

Stevenson J, Graham P, Fredman G, McLaughun V (1987) A twin study of genetic influences on reading and spelling ability and disability. *J Child Psychol* **28**: 229–47.

Swan D, Goswami U (1997) Phonological awareness deficits in developmental dyslexia and the phonological representations hypothesis. *J Exp Child Psychol* **66**: 18–41.

Thomson ME (1975) Laterality and reading: a research note. *Br J Education Psychol* **45**: 313–21.

Thomson ME (1976) Laterality effects in dyslexics and controls using verbal dichotic listening tasks. *Neuropsychologia* **14**: 243–6.

Thomson ME (1977) Individual differences in the acquisition of written language: an integrated model and its implications for dyslexia. PhD Thesis, University of Aston.

Thomson ME (1979) The nature of written language. In: Newton MJ, Thomson ME, Richards IR, eds, *Readings in Dyslexia: A Study Text to Accompany the Aston Index*. Wisbech: Learning Development Aids.

Thomson ME (1990) *Developmental Dyslexia*, 3rd edn. London: Whurr Publishers.

Thomson ME, Newton MJ (1979) A concurrent validity study of the Aston Index. In: Newton MJ, Thomson ME, Richards IR, eds, *Readings in Dyslexia: A Study Text to Accompany the Aston Index*. Wisbech: Learning Development Aids.

Thomson ME, Watkins EJ (1999) *Dyslexia: A teaching handbook,* 2nd edn. London: Whurr Publishers.

Thomson ME, Wilsher C (1979) Some aspects of memory in dyslexics and controls. In: Gruneberg M, Morris P, Sykes R, eds, *Practical Aspects of Memory.* London: Academic Press.

Tizard Report, Department of Education and Science (1972) *Report of the Advisory Committee on Handicapped Children.* London: HMSO.

Vellutino FR (1979) *Dyslexia – Theory and Research.* Cambridge, MA: The MIT Press.

Vellutino FR, Steger JA, Desetto L, Phillips F (1975) Immediate and delayed recognition of visual stimuli in poor and normal readers. *J Exp Child Psychol* **19**: 223–32.

Waddington CH (1957) *The Strategy of Genes.* London: George Allen & Unwin.

Wechsler D (1992) *The Wechsler Intelligence Scale for Children III.* Sidcup: Psychological Corporation.

Wechsler Objective Reading Dimensions (1993) Sidcup: Psychological Corporation.

Wilkinson GS (1993) *The Wide Range Achievement Test,* 3rd edn (WRAT-3) Wilmington, DE: Wide Range.

Yule W (1967) Predicting reading ages on Neale Analysis of Reading Ability. *Br J Educational Psychol* **37**: 252–5.

Yule W, Rutter M, Berger M, Thomson J (1974) Over and under achievement in reading: distribution in the general population. *Br J Educational Psychol* **44**: 1–12.

Zurif EF, Carson G (1970) Dyslexia in relation to cerebral dominance and temporal analysis. *Neuropsychologia* **8**: 351–61.

Index

Franklin Pierce College Library

00140899